LAURA ANTONIOU ON MI[

There's a certain freedom that comes wi[
The most obvious perk is the ability to st[
and remind people, "it ain't real - these[
This excuses me from the weight of the biography, who
have facts and numbers and research behind them. I get to be inaccurate,
mistaken, I get to exaggerate, dilute, even create characters and situations
which seem wildly surreal, or difficult to believe. Hey, it's just my fantasies!

And then, one day, someone said, "I love how you captured Midori in the
character of Ken Mandarin."

I said, quite memorably, "Who?"

Maybe it was the few years I spent out of the greater scene, writing books,
investigating religion, going through community detox... I admit I somehow
missed ever actually meeting Midori until 1999. And I was somewhat
perplexed by two things. For one, Ken Mandarin is, to put it bluntly, one of my
less realistic creations, a Eurasian heiress, an unapologetic hedonist, a multi-
lingual sexual chameleon in fabulous clothing who is equally at home among
millionaires and we mundane working class pervs. And secondly, I kept hearing
from more people who agreed - Ken Mandarin was a great depiction of Midori!

When more than two people in the scene agree on something like that, you know
there's a certain surreality to the situation. Imagine my surprise when I finally did
meet the real life Midori - in Atlanta, I think - and one of the first things we did was
have a laugh at the people who were so mistaken. As either of us could tell you,
Midori is part Japanese. Ken Mandarin, the fictional character is part Chinese.

Sheesh, that's a world of difference!

However, the unapologetic hedonist at home in the world, who wears stunning
fetish couture? OK, that part does seem to match. Now, of only someone would
make Midori an heiress...maybe she'd share it with me. But in the meantime, I enjoy
her company, her wit, her sheer sexiness and of course, her wise advice, tempered
with good humor and realism and flavored with skillful touch of sheer romance.

Midori is a refreshing and needed voice to the alternative sexuality community-
unashamed and joyful, funny and ironic, honest and pragmatic. And then, when
you least expect it, she'll hit you upside the head with a stirring description of a
fetish, a scene or sexual encounter, and you realize, she really loves this. She has a
hard-on for all this stuff - the clothing, the rituals, the pleasures and the agonies. And
like any lover, she knows the realistic limitations of the SM/leather/kink scene.

For me, the fiction writer, that makes all the difference in the world. Anyone can make up stories, layer lies over truth; I'm proof of that. It takes a romantic realist to make the truth exciting, dangerous, sexy, thrilling, lusty. And luckily, we have one, for real. Purchase her, read her, nod and learn and smile. Then impress your friends by knowing truth from fiction. Or, impress your next date. Midori would approve.

Laura Antoniou, author of *The Marketplace*
2005

MORE PRAISE FOR WILD SIDE SEX:

Very few sex educators combine down-to-earth knowledge with out-of-this world sex appeal as effectively as Midori. The universe of kink is a better, hotter, more intelligent place with her in it.
Janet Hardy, co-author, *The New Topping Book*, *The New Bottoming Book*, *Radical Ecstasy*

Already established as the world's best-known expert and writer on the subject of erotic rope bondage, San Francisco's SM queen Midori now promises to repeat that success across a broad range of pervy topics with this collection of essays on every aspect of kink. Written in her familiar erudite and personable style, these pieces offer an engaging blend of practical information and advice, frank revelation and unabashed titillation that will not only get dedicated kinksters' juices flowing, but also spark the imagination of even the most mildly curious mainstream reader. If ever anyone deserves the title of Thinking Person's Pervert, it is Midori!

Tony Mitchell Editor, *Skin Two* Magazine

This book is not only the advanced version of the *Joy of Sex* for those interested in exploring BDSM, but a very good description of and introduction to the BDSM world. Midori, explains the nuances of BDSM better than anyone else has. I expect many people will read this book as an entry into the BDSM lifestyle, but many human sexuality courses also will assign it to give the student the flavor of BDSM sexuality and the associated lifestyle. I heartily recommend this book.

Charles Moser, Ph.D., M.D., *Sex Disasters (And how to Survive Them)*

WILD SIDE SEX:

Photo by Steve Diet Goedde

WILD SIDE SEX:
The Book of Kink
Educational, Sensual, and Entertaining Essays

By Midori

 Daedalus Publishing Company

This trade paperback is published by

Daedalus Publishing
2807 W. Sunset Boulevard
Los Angeles, CA 90026`
www.daedaluspublishing.com

First Edition: 2005
ISBN: 1-881943-22-4

Edited by Linda Santiman

Cover Photo & Inside Photos by Steve Diet Goedde

Manufactured in the United States of America

ACKNOWLEDGEMENTS

Thank you to all the wonderful sexual adventurers, erotic pioneers and pleasure seekers who came before me. Without you, this would be a really boring and joyless world.

There are many wonderful people who encouraged me in thinking and writing about wickedly fun sex. My editor, Linda Santiman from Daedalus Publishing deserves special thanks for her encouragement, patience, and creative reminders and for the general ass kicking she did to get me to finish this book. Thanks to the proof readers who helped me polish the book and smooth out the material, Andrea Zanin, Alaska Roy, Maraina and Gregg.

My gratitude goes to all those who in the past have encouraged me to write. Without you, this book wouldn't exist: Layne Winklebleck, Kat Sunlove and Dara of *Spectator* magazine. Tony Mitchell and Tim Woodward of *Skin Two* magazine. Diana Cage of *On Our Backs* magazine. The unsinkable and ever funny Ernest Greene and Ira Levine. Dr. William Henkin for his wisdom and insights. Cecilia Tan of Circlet Press who endures my slow writing and strange humor. Janet Hardy of Greenery Press for taking a chance on me. Phil F. for being my sounding board on so many of these essays.

I am indebted to those in my life and communities that have taught and influenced me. First, to all the men and women of the leather community who have died of HIV/AIDS/HRC. You shouldn't have died so young. I miss you all. And now for the living... my teachers.... Dr. Carol Queen and Dr. Robert Lawrence for their seductive ways. Dr. Annie Sprinkle for her joyous energy. Laura Antoniou and Karen Tayler, dear friends and two of the funniest storytellers I know. Joseph Bean - the twinkle in his eyes makes me giggle. Kim Airs of Grand Opening Boutique who's the big sister that every one wishes they could have. Karen Mendalson for getting me started on this whole kink teaching path. Michael Manning for so much erotic inspiration.

My sincere appreciation to the Leather Archive and Museum for keeping our history and memory alive. Thanks to the National Coalition for Sexual Freedom for their work to promote the individuals' right to sexual self-determination.

Lastly to my family... my mother and grandmother. They did not merely set the example, they were the example, providing the leadership I needed to live life honestly and to follow a passion, even on the roads less traveled.

Most importantly my beloved partner, Kelly. Without your love, patience and devotion, I would not be so happy and fulfilled in life.

Midori, May, 2005

Photo by Steve Diet Goedde

CONTENTS

BEFORE WE BEGIN...

I love sex. I love to do it. I love to look at it. I love to talk about it. I love to think about it and I love to write about it. I've been writing about sex for so long now that, honestly, I had forgotten about how I got started until I started editing this book and tried to remember where it all began. But here's the story... I was in my mid 20's. At that time, I wasn't enmeshed with any of the organized kink communities, but I was an eager visitor to many sectors of the San Francisco sexual underground. San Francisco Sex Information, a free sexual information hotline and resource center, had given me some of the most innovative and thorough human sexuality education available – at 60 + hours of education, I had been exposed to 30 times more sex educator training then most newly minted physicians. This training and my desire to make something of that knowledge landed me a job with a very large sex toy mail-order company. As one of my work duties I started writing pithy little sex advice columns in the intra-company filled with product info and merchandise sales tips for the sales people. They weren't meant for the general public, but intended as little throwaway pieces for a tiny, closed-list group. Little did I know that fifteen years later, I'd be traveling the world teaching classes in adventurous sex, and writing about the many things I've learned... and about my own personal journeys as well.

In this book you'll find a collection of my writings from 1997 to 2005. These writings include my thoughts on sex, observations about kinky people, my personal erotic delights, sweet confessions, illuminations of my darker moments and bits of fun and useful advice that I've given my friends. Many of the essays were written for kink magazines, smut publications and people who come to my seminars, so the language is very sexual. Sometimes I use language or vernacular common to a specific community. In putting this book together I've tried my best to make minimal changes to the original text, but I have inserted explanations of some terms and updated information. For a few pieces I fleshed out thoughts that were not fully developed at the time of their original writing. Revisiting my old essays was quite entertaining. It was almost like reading through a diary. Memories of old lovers, new discoveries and passions flooded my mind, making it hard form time to time, to do the objective task of editing.

This book is for the seasoned sexual adventurers as well as those new to the path of sexual exploration. My writing is grouped into four sections. Two of them cover the psychological foundations of consensual erotic sadomasochism, dominance and submission. One section is dedicated to fetishism and the mind of the fetishist. The last section is a collection of short little how-to's on specific fun kinky sex techniques. You don't need to read the sections or essays in order. Please feel free to skip around and read the topics that interest you the most. Or if you just want to get insight into those weird things other people do, then go to the ones that baffle you the most!

If you are new to kinky sex, you might want to go directly to "Part 4: Tips & Tricks for Adventurous Sex". Try them out in the bedroom and go from there. If you want further information on good basics and techniques of kinky sex, there are a lot of great books, classes and resources out there. I mention a number of appropriate resources in the individual how-to pieces. You'll also find a list of my recommended books on my web site at www.fhp-inc.com. I try to update that list whenever I come across a good resource.

Many of you will be relieved that I wrote the bulk of these essays for the experienced perv and not for the absolute beginner. Some topics may be edgy, challenging or perhaps even scary to some of you. I debated whether or not to include certain essays. In the end, I decided to go for it. There are enough basic information sources out there but not enough non-fiction aimed at seasoned kinksters. As a result, much of this book is for you.

So why should new adventurers read this stuff? Some of you may think it's irresponsible for me to share my thoughts about more advanced sorts of play with novice explorers. Now, let's be honest. Did you always do the sensible things that parents and authority figures advised you to? I believe everyone should have the opportunity to look into the hidden corners of sexual delight and learn from others. Why should you have to blindly explore when an essay or two, a class or two and some shared experiences could prevent you from making unnecessary mistakes, suffering doubts and experiencing less-then-great sex?

You might find an essay in here that explains what you've been feeling about something. Great! Bookmark that essay and pass it on to your lover. Maybe you'll find a technique that you want to share with your playmate. Wonderful! Read that piece together and create variations. Does something in this book upset you? Good. Rant about it to others and see what comes of that debate.

Use this book and stories from my personal life in any way you see fit to improve your sex life. That's why I wrote it. If all else fails, you can always use this book as a spanking paddle.

Wishing you steamy nights full of erotic adventures,

Midori

Part One: Fundamentals of Kink

Photo by Steve Diet Goedde

Why SM?

I do SM in search of a moment's clarity and pureness of existence. In the act of SM and D/s I shed layers. I shed the layers of calcified defenses and starched propriety and peel away my civilized veneer. In the act of SM and D/s I must be fully present in the moment. There's no other choice. No other way for me to live leather. Anything less would be an act of self-disrespect and dishonor.... A sham. At the beginning of a scene I may not always know what I will find under those layers. Under my sense of my socially acceptable self, I may find an entirely unexpected and naked soul looking back at me.

I have flown with wings of ecstasy on clouds of laughter and joy. I have plunged deep into the oceans of tears and sorrows found in all grieving hearts. I have tapped the fountain of eternal compassion within me. I have crawled through the thorns of hate sprouting from my own bile. I have touched the peace of universal love. I have loved you, my lover, so hard that I wanted to tear you from limb to limb and devour you whole. My flesh has twisted into a creature of lust, a demon of desire and a god of blissful nothingness.

In stepping into the arena of a SM experience, I step knowingly into a dimension where lies and false intentions may turn around and bite me back like a poorly handled bullwhip. When I play, I must be honest to my hungers. I must give my inner beasts room to feed, even if they've not yet fully emerged. My flesh becomes a vehicle of expression for these naked and hungry beasts, the rawest parts of my soul.

Passion rules my play.

In the moment of SM, nothing else matters. Only this I know to be true; that there is only me, my partner and the world formed by the two of us. Even in the midst of a crowded play party, the crowd simply becomes the backdrop and the grand chorus for the unfolding primal drama. They bear witness to the sublime arias.

This theater of desire is not a stage of façade, but rather a place where the façade is removed. We use the conventions of roles to remove the masks of the daily roles we've allowed ourselves to become. It's a nakedness that we are not accustomed to. To be barefaced like this is to expose all of the self: the strength, the beauty, the frightening and the frailty. We expose this naked self to the world, to those who bear witness, to our partner and, most frighteningly, to ourselves. We've spent so many years constructing a sense of self with the complex interweaving of inner character, parental molding, social sanctions and disapproval, that we fear that such moments of soulful nakedness might, perhaps, unravel for all eternity this carefully, delicately crafted identity. What then? What's beyond that event horizon?

It is only a leap of faith that can take us to that realm of honest nakedness.

The unknown frightens us. The fear of the unknown and of the pain of change may keep our feet nailed to our lack of fulfillment. Better, some may say, a comfortable discontent than an uncertain bliss. Better to toil the unyielding earth than to fly too close to the sun, as we might fall again.

More tragic, perhaps, than those who have never flown, are those who fly and yet do not feel the heat of their passion's sun scorching their back. I have seen some people's eyes, a cold, numb glaze of habitual play. The whip flies with grace and precision, but I cannot sense the heart. Why do they play? What do they seek in the moment of play? Who are they playing for? For the thirst of their desires and love of the union in that moment... or for the approval of others? Are they feeding an inner hunger, or do they go forever feeling, somehow, hollow?

These hungry ghosts may be endowed with skill. They haunt the play world with flourish and judgment. They are often the arbiters of what's deemed proper play, the definers of the *corpus juris* of leather. They see young initiates, tearing into each other with unsurpassed passion and raw desire, flying in their private skyscape. Will the heat these lovers generate incite any awe in these arbiters? Or will the judges simply deconstruct their technical failings?

May we never forget our uninitiated hearts and passions.

A SM moment shared may touch you indelibly. It may stay with you eternally and you may be forever changed. The moment may be as fleeting as spring rains in the desert, but the joy it feeds and the flowers of pleasure it brings to bloom are just as brilliant as a desert rose.

How can I forget the magic of opening the doors to the darkest part of someone's child-heart despite their life-weary body? I will always treasure the beauty and the art that we create with rope and flesh. The symphony of pain and pleasure that we conduct will always echo in my mind. With a consenting other I can unleash my monsters to commit the atrocities of passion. The deep impact of these moments feeds an eternal flame in me that keeps my lust for life blazing bright.

With this eternal flame, I may warm my soul on the bone chilling days of the lonely heart. While this flame stays lit, I might go for a long period without playing. I shall not play for the sole reason of obligation or expectation. I shall play only as my passion moves me to play. I shall enter into the moments of SM to feed an honest hunger, and not for the sake of wonton and destructive gluttony.

I do SM in search of the moment's clarity and pureness of existence.

Public Sex

I push her lithe little body up against the cold tile wall. She grasps the steel handicap railing with her right hand as I throw her left leg over my arm. She lets out a moan as I bite into her neck. My hands are busy unbuttoning her silk blouse, releasing her firm breasts. Impatient with the skirt I rip it off and toss it aside. I had her pull her panties off earlier while she frantically sucked my dick. She's now exposed, with her shaved cunt hungrily open to me in its full wet and naked glory to me. I look back over my shoulder to make sure that I locked the stall door. The music pounds through the floor and up our feet into our entwined bodies, right into our beating cunts. I know I'm soaking wet and I can see her cunt dripping. Somewhere in a dark, piss reeking bathroom of a San Francisco fetish club I'm taking my sweet submissive baby and fucking her deep to the rhythm of vintage Nine Inch Nails... "I wanna' fuck you like an animal..."

So, now you know one of my favorite past times: public sex and public SM.

How long has it been since you parked in a dark parking lot, crawled into the back seat of your car and fucked until the windows started to drip with condensation? Do you remember the thrill of copping a feel and getting a blowjob in the den at your parent's house? How about the naughty rush of getting it on in your dorm room and trying to keep quiet so you wouldn't catch hell from your roommate sleeping just a few feet away? Did you ever sneak a hottie into your frat house or sorority house for a little forbidden fornication?

It's fun to get away with it, isn't it?

Of course when we were first making out in parked cars and screwing behind the stadium it was out of necessity created by lack of private space. Now that we're all grown up, we have our own homes and a regular paycheck, we can always play sex and SM games at home or rent a hotel room.

Just because you're grown up now and have your own little love pad doesn't mean that you can't enjoy the thrills of a public scene anymore – let the Fetish Diva give you some kinky tips.

I.   First you should consider why it is that you want play in public.

Your motivation and purpose will help to shape your deviously lusty plans. You have to think about why you're doing what you're doing in public: after all, it would be so much more convenient in the comfort of your own home. Does the public nature of it in itself turn you on? Does the bit of increased embarrassment and humiliation you and your partner may endure make you hard or wet? Is your partner an exhibitionist? Do you get a sexual rush from the fear of getting caught? Maybe you like having a secret from the world? Do you, as a dominant, get a hard-on from controlling your bottom's reactions in public? Do you get off on making her wet or making her come in inappropriate places? Do you, as a submissive, find an erotic charge in the unknown element of your partner's plans? Do you delight in finding out how adventurous your partner can be?

Candi, the grrl that I fucked in the smelly club bathroom stall, is a shy exhibitionist and a wickedly delicious submissive. There's a whole lot that she won't do on her own that she'll do under my command. Obeying my erotic whims turns her on. Being teased by me makes her wet. She comes quickly when I make her do nasty little things for my amusement. It blows her mind when I force her to come in public and in inappropriate places. In turn I enjoy being given that much control and power over her sexuality and behavior. I want to see how much she'll do for me. Power turns me on. So, that's our motivation.

19

I've made her masturbate under the table at a crowded sushi restaurant and then had her lick her own fingers clean. I've had her kiss my boots on my front door steps in broad daylight. I've ordered her to lick my pussy clean in an alley while I leaned back on the vibrating wall of a nightclub.

Sometimes the motivation is strictly about cashing in on an opportunity or the lack of more conventional locations. Once upon a time I was at a chi-chi country club fitness center. I had a chance to slide into a one-woman sized shower stall with this Brazilian goddess and make the bucking two-headed sea monster with her. You bet I took the opportunity! In order to keep quiet we figured out that it was best to keep our lips and tongues interlocked and the shower on full blast during the whole experience.

So why do *you* do it in public?

II.   Next you need to figure out the potential risks and limits involved.

After all, part of the thrill of public scenes is the risk. If public play was perfectly accepted and risk free, it wouldn't be half as exciting, would it? I may want to bend Candi over the hood of my car, pull her panties down and fist her in a parking lot off Fisherman's Wharf, but I consider the challenges involved before I actually grab the lube.

Some risks are very real. For example, public exposure and lewd and lascivious behaviors are defined by local ordinances and punishable by law to varying degrees of severity. Most of us don't want to end up in jail with a rap sheet just for one night of thrill seeking sex. So, how much are you going to push the local laws? I live in San Francisco, a pretty libertine city where the cops have seen just about everything. I can do a lot more here than I could in some small Bible Belt town. In San Francisco I'd probably look for a dark corner in a less frequented parking garage or an off hour construction site to reduce the risk of arrest and prosecution. But in a small Bible Belt town I might take her waaaay out to the woods to bend her over the hood of my car, hundreds of miles from any good citizens, sheriffs or park rangers. Then again, I'd be a little worried about those survivalist types. Remember the couple who was hiking in the Blue Ridge Mountains and was shot by some redneck for having sex outside of their tent? In the end, you have to be the judge of how much risk is too much risk. You're an adult. The laws and the consequences are real. Figure it out.

The biggest legal risk I took was a quickie hand-fucking with a boyfriend in a phone booth across the street from a police station. Now that was a thrill!

Other risks are about pushing social boundaries of what's considered acceptable behavior in a given community. San Francisco has a great event called the Folsom Street Fair. Thousands of perverts and kinksters - primarily gay, but many straight and bi folks as well, gather every year for an open-air celebration of BDSM and the Leather life. Here people walk around half naked, sometimes fully nude, collared, chained, bound and being whipped while police stroll by protecting the safety of these very same collared and whipped citizens. No one is going to notice me leading Candi down the street with a leash or even making her suck my silicone dick. (They may object to public real-dick sucking. I'm not sure.) The only thing I'd have to worry about there is her blow job technique being critiqued by the leathermen. But I don't think I can do that in Fargo without being brutally beaten up. There are things that I would consider doing in a dark theater but not at my date's corporate holiday party.

Your own reputation aside, you should also be considerate and respectful of people that didn't directly agree to play with you, but unwittingly have come to play a part in your scene. I'm talking about the people in the environment around you. They didn't consent to having a scene with the two of you, so try your best to leave them out of it. If I want to tie Candi up in a public restroom, I have to consider whether the people coming into the bathroom would want to see this happening. Unless this is at The Eagle or La Nouvelle Justine, (a now-defunct SM restaurant in New York City), probably not. So, what do I do? Instead of tying her up in the open area of the rest room, I'll drag her into the stall and do it there. Whether you're comfortable with other people seeing two pairs of feet is up to you. Remember, you are probably still breaking the law.

Sometimes pushing the social norm may be just the hottest thing you can do. Gay clubs with back rooms or black rooms are often used for flagrant public sex. That's part of the attraction. When you're a

21

woman, much less a nosebleed-high-femme, the risk is that shameless pussy sex in a fag bar can make some of the more uppity guys nervous, getting you kicked out in the end. I love playing with the balance of cool/not-cool. So, of course I go for it.

One night at the Lure (RIP) in NYC I sauntered in wearing my full female US Army officer's uniform, high heels and all, with Boi X in tow. Boi X was looking sharp in latex chaps and tank. At least the boys could deal with a pair of leather women strolling through. Not long after, I had Boi X on hir back on the beer soaked stone floor with me standing, straddling over hir. Shi didn't know that I never wear panties with skirts. (Why bother?) Next thing you know, I felt the orgasmic relief of hot golden fluid rushing out of me. It hit hir latex loudly and shi moaned even more loudly as shi realized what was happening to hir. I think shi came. When I was done I just walked away and let hir steep in a pool of my piss, hir cum, hir sweat and stale beer. The guys got a kick out of the show. Of course, they didn't actually have to see any female parts, so that made it easier for them.

Another late night at My Place, where furtive looking men cruised the back room looking to hook up with a trick, I occupied a corner ledge dolled up as a Nelly-boy-gentlemen. To my left was a fag daddy friend of mine who was whispering in my ear what a sexy boy I made. I liked turning him on despite his Kinsey 5.9 status. In front of me were my rough little butch boi and the daddy's handsome, greedy pig boy. My boi could suck my dick better than the bio-boi, creating a nasty little dick-sucking competition. Men were cruising by - curious, aroused, disturbed and somehow shaken up.

Since you're going to have at least one person in a potentially very vulnerable and compromising situation, I don't suggest that you risk basic safety. You probably don't want to do a public scene in a high crime area. There's also Mother Nature to consider. I know someone who had the very sexy idea to tie down his lover with tent stakes in a field while camping in the wilderness. The ants did not appreciate that steamy sex scene on top of their nest. The girlfriend was bitten pretty severely. It's also good idea to know the difference between a good branch to use as a switch and poison oak. Truth is more foolish than fiction.

While many public play ideas are fun and quite possible to carry out, you need to be aware that some fantasies are best kept as just that - a fantasy. These scenarios you should keep for your dirty storytelling, steamy phone sex sessions and on-line chat room encounters. Or read them in *Black Sheets* magazine by seriously bent writers.

III - **Now, let's get to the good stuff! Let's talk about all the juicy action you can get up to in public scenes.**

Feeling a bit shy still about public scenes? Here are several modest, yet very exciting ideas. I've combined them into one full evening, but you can certainly use any part of it or mix and match the ideas. For the sake of this fantasy, let's assume that you're the dominant partner, or the party planner if you prefer not to identify as dom or sub. Here I describe the bottom as a gal, but it could very well be a guy. You only need to make some minor mental adjustments for the parts.

Plan to go out for dinner. Before you go out, have her kneel before you and place a collar on her. This can be as simple as a ribbon tied around her neck or a full leather slave collar. Throughout the entire evening she'll be very conscious of being collared to you. A decorative rope body harness under her clothing is another way to keep her aware of her submission to you. Use a thinner rope so it's not bulky to interfere with fashion or too tight to cause any difficulty with circulation. Now you need to pack a few things. Put together a small bag with a vaginal or anal plug, Ben Wa balls, lube and maybe a condom for the butt plug option. Also sneak into your coat pocket a blindfold, scissors, cable tie - or what's referred to as riot cuffs - as well as a small "bullet" style vibrator or a cordless remote control vibrator. Long drives are always fun: once you're in the car, have her disrobe slowly until her sex is perhaps more is fully exposed. Seatbelts act as excellent bondage devices. After all, it's illegal not to wear one, right? Place the blindfold on her. If you don't want to look to other drivers like you just kidnapped a person, take a pair of those fully wrapping sunglasses and paint them black. You could let your fingers to the walking or make her play with herself. (Goddess forbid, I would never suggest you do anything that compromises your driving skills!) The blindfold adds the thrill of vulnerability and the thrill of not knowing who's watching her. There may not be any other drivers seeing this, but she'll only know what you tell her!

When you get to the restaurant, you can pass a small bag of goodies to her. You may choose to give the order verbally or in a letter included in the bag. Imagine, a cutesy, fluffy Hallmark or Hello Kitty card with the dirtiest words and instructions! She's to go to the bathroom, cover the butt plug with a condom, lube it up and put it in her ass and return to the table. If you've got a yen for high tech sex toys you can order her to insert a cordless remote control vibrator or high-end electrical toys such as ErosTek in her pussy or ass and return to the table. Of course you have the controls. (By the way, if you use one of the remote control options, and someone at another table yelps when you press the button… then just look over to them and flash a knowing grin! Many of these sex toy remotes are set at the same frequency.) From this beginning, the possibilities are endless.

Of course, there are all sorts of other ways to have public fun. Secret foot worship can happen anywhere... for example, I have fond memories of a stolen moment of toe sucking in the back of a cab as I and a kinky guy friend named Shoe Boy rushed towards a Broadway show in the Big Apple.

Once I took Candi with me to Foot Worship, a San Francisco fetish shoe shop. The owner was kind enough to leave us alone after delivering a stack of new shoes for me to consider. She sat on a footstool as she helped me try shoes on. I took advantage of the position and her short skirt to press my stocking clad foot on her panty-covered pussy. She began to slowly grind onto my pretty foot, all the while blushing. Before long she was wildly humping my leg. At the end of it all, she decided that she liked the pointy toe pumps. I purchased the shoes and later had her give me a personal shoe fucking show at home. (If you do this sort of thing, please remember to be considerate to the shopkeepers. Don't slime the shoes you aren't buying!)

I've enjoyed lots of other public wickedness with my submissives. Golden shower scenes can work just as well in a truck stop bathroom as in a deserted construction area, or even a fancy restaurant. I can always return from the bathroom holding my white wine glass nonchalantly, and pass the "wine" to my sub. Healthy pee looks like white wine. A high-rise hotel window is a great place to play out the hidden fantasies of a reluctant exhibitionist. Cruel and seductive words of dominance whispered in a crowded elevator may elicit a response requiring serious self-control. The submissive gets all cranked up and has to deal with their hard-on or gushing cunt in public. And for the subs, lest you think that these games are just for dominants to initiate—let me assure you that nasty whispers from a bottom to a top, or a pair of wet panties passed discreetly by a submissive to her dominant, can set a top's heart throbbing, not to mention give their libido a boost!

SM play clubs, swing clubs and sex clubs are good places for nasty, down and dirty screwing and kink action in front of anyone who cares to watch... and if you like the idea of somebody jacking off to your show, this may be the perfect opportunity. You can turn yourself into an amateur peep show! (Watch but don't touch is safe sex, after all!) And everyone consented that sex might be happening there. Strip joints are great for playing with turn on, humiliation and exhibition. Ever force someone to pay to confess his or her dirty fantasies to a bombshell dancer? Ever pay a hooker or a hustler boy just to watch you have sex?

Ahhh, the pleasures of depravity are endless!

Pleasure, Pain, Dominance & Submission

Pleasure and Pain

Scientists have found that pleasure and pain are related. I read this in a recent news article and chuckled. We could have told them that! I wonder if this means that we the erotic sado-masochists are one step closer to being scientifically legitimized, or one step closer to being placed into some form of curative therapy for a physically based neural disorder. (Remember that forced and elective electroshock therapy as a "cure" for homosexuality was a perfectly legitimate prescription even within the last thirty years or so.) While the latter is a mighty scary thought, I suppose if the religious extremists and the pharmaceutical industries were to have their way, there could be a distasteful outcome.

A study released in the December 6th, 2001 issue of Neuron journal reports the finding that the brain structures previously described as reward-associated circuitry is also activated, if differently, by pain. (Becerra, L. et al. "Reward Circuitry Activation by Noxious Thermal Stimuli". Neuron, vol. 32, 6 December 2001. 927-946.) The Massachusetts General Hospital study led by Dr. David Borsook is primarily concerned with the issues of understanding neural response to the very subjective experience of pain, and focuses on the effective treatment of chronic pain. The study established, among other things, that the neural responses to pain are caused both by physical and emotional sensations. In a cheesy attempt to sex up an otherwise bone-dry topic, CNN.com asked Dr. Borsook to speculate about sadomasochists. He casually hypothesized that there could be a potential for the pain/reward circuitry to have been somehow modified for the kinky population group.

I guess now they can finally explain this phenomenon: the intense masochist steps off the cross, with shredded flesh from an unrelenting single tail. He's beaming with pleasure and delight. Suddenly he winces and says "ouch!" upon stubbing his toe on the edge of the cross.

Dominance and Submission

D/s: Dominance & submission. M/s: Master & slave. Maybe it's my misperception, but it seems to me that the topic of D/s and M/s has come back into vogue the last couple of years among the polite society of kink. In 1999, when I attended the remarkable "International Masters and slaves Together" weekend conference in Atlanta, it still seemed like men and women who sought the path of mastery and slavery were pretty much considered eccentric by the bulk of the contemporary pervy folk. You know, much like that crazy uncle that everyone tolerates, but doesn't quite understand. That seems less the case today. (For the sake of this essay I'll be discussing D/s and M/s in similar terms. Let me apologize in advance for the limitations of language. D/s and M/s may mean different things to you and your relationship. Relational dynamics are highly subjective, so if I seem to mix the two or differently define these terms then you do, please forgive me.)

Maybe it's a generational cycle. We lost a great deal of knowledge, experience and continuity within the leather community due to the ravages of HIV / AIDS. This created a chasm of knowledge and experience. Then, the advent of the Internet also brought a huge influx of new kinky adventurers into the community. Perhaps we have come to a place in a cycle of generational growth where the foundations of the physical experiences of SM have been adequately covered. Perhaps that's leading many now to consider and explore the potential of the deeply emotional and human relationships within a kinky social construct.

If this is the case, then it's a worthy pursuit. I suppose we could look at it as sort of a hierarchy of need of SM. First, like a child learning to walk, we make our first steps into the community, connect with others and learn that we are not alone in the world. Then we learn the basics of communal language and social navigation. The period of discovery of our own desires might be compared to the necessary self-absorption of the pre-adult. That's followed by a period of learning the physical skills, like basic bondage and fundamentals of flogging. I suppose that's like learning to drive, dating and figuring out how to do our own laundry. Then with early adulthood, we begin to explore our relationship to the rest of the world and how to form our own social and familial structure. We learn to tackle more complex social interactions around subjective topics. I wonder if this is a good analogy for the recent surge of discussion on polyamory, D/s, Master/slave dynamics, and other alternative relationship forms.

On the other hand, what if the current fascination with D/s stems from naivete or escapism? The world is a very complicated and often chaotic place. Many feel out of control, helpless or overwhelmed in today's society. The written and unwritten rules of conduct of generations past, prejudices and power boundaries that served as the glue holding society together, have given way to seeming social disorder, where no one is certain of the rules. There is no "sure thing" anymore.

Don't misunderstand me. I will never have a problem with a civil world where people strive to behave with grace and consideration. What I am concerned with here is with people who are investing energy into dominance and submission in hopes that it will somehow fix their problems. Abdication of power in formalized D/s or M/s does not make the helplessness or powerlessness that the individual feels in the world go away. Taking control of someone else's life as a dominant or master doesn't suddenly create order and control in your life where there seemed to be none before. In these cases, the original problems only fester faster and deeper under the pretty, pervy Band-Aid called D/s.

I see many people enter into D/s relationships with great enthusiasm, dreaming of days and nights of whips, chains and nubile slave girls. Don't get me wrong, I think that's a great and romantic goal to aspire to. Heck, can I get that too? Unfortunately I also see them slinking out of the same relationship at the first sign of communication stress or erotic disillusionment. In some cases I've seen people switch from one "committed 24/7 D/s" relationship to the next as fast as teenage dating.

It's easy to understand the source of disillusionment. Stories like *Exit to Eden, Claiming of Sleeping Beauty* and *The Story of O* make D/s look really appealing and super sexy to any perv living in the real world. I would love to wake up one morning in a castle, surrounded by beautiful and willing slaves that I may use and abuse as I see fit, while not having to ever work again or worry about the pedestrian issues of life. While a *Story of O* scenario can be sustained for an evening, and perhaps for several days in a row, it's most likely to start to show deep cracks on the pretty veneer after a while, as the stresses of real life creep in. Mowing the lawn because you're told to is not always sexy. Dealing with the medical care industry is hardly a hard-on. But these are things that have to get dealt with, even in M/s relationships.

In discussing D/s and M/s there's often a failure of discussion between the distinction of sexual D/s and relational D/s. Sexual D/s is where the primary focus is surrender and control of sexual power and erotic behavior, most often within a sensual encounter bound by time and space. Relational D/s is where the primary focus is on the hierarchy of authority and decision-making that encompasses the relationship between two (or more) people, who each operate fully in a complex world. The relationship is also assumed to exist in the real world. A sexual D/s situation might contain relational D/s only for the duration in which the sexual power is surrendered and it may cease the moment that the sexual dynamic is no longer the central focus of those involved. Conversely, relational D/s may have little or no sexual component to it, or sex may serve as an integral yet not overwhelming aspect of the relationship.

Sexual D/s is the flashy stuff that's easy to write steamy stories about and get absorbed into watching at SM gatherings and sex parties. It's also much easier to grasp at a superficial level. Some couples' sexual D/s relationship may be predicated on a temporary removal from real world concerns. There's nothing wrong with that if there's a realistic expectations around the temporal limitations of that from of D/s at that level of erotic intensity. Unfortunately some fail to recognize that these very traits that make sexual D/s so hot, also make it really difficult to sustain in the form of a relationship over an extended period of time with the same original rigor. For some, relational D/s may also come with great and constant pomp, formality, ritual, and dozens and dozens of stances and protocols, remembered by number for sitting and standing and whatnot. From what I have seen, these tend to burn up in flames as quickly as the intense sexual D/s relationships. On the other hand, those D/s relationships that have practical flexibility within the scope of real life seem to be able to sustain relational D/s for longer.

Functional relational D/s, like the brown-frocked plane Jane, may not catch the eyes of the dungeon thrill-seeker, but it seems to have greater potential for longevity, as it's generally designed around mutual affection, service and the common tasks of the everyday. Where the problems seem to manifest in these relationships is when the people

29

involved get buried under all the weight of the chores of real life, when the original purpose of the intentionally-entered-into D/s relationship gets lost. It crumbles under the pressures of the mundane, leaving one or all parties vaguely resentful and unfulfilled.

What all this boils down to is that D/s and M/s relationships are very real human relationships, and thus come with the potential for great joys of the heart and soul and all the heartaches to boot. It takes a whole lot of work and clarity on the part of everyone involved to define and execute their contributions and responsibilities.

Here's how I defined D/s relationship for a discussion group and class that I facilitated:

> *D/s is a relationship construct containing elements of formalized power distribution, entered into with mutual agreement by two or more self-sufficient and responsible adults possessing their own power and identity.*

I really feel that it's important for all the parties entering into a D/s relationship to possess their own set of tools for self-sufficiency and a well-formed sense of the Self. Otherwise, the relationship entered into might become the framework for co-dependency, mutual escapism and blame.

One must possess oneself, and that self must have strength and substance before it can be surrendered as something worth holding. One must have self-knowledge and self-control before deeply knowing another person and being granted control of them. Both must communicate as fully mature beings. Beyond these points, all other elements become variables by which each relationship is defined....

Modern Chivalry: The Romance of D/s:

I am a sado-masochist. A dominant sadist, to be precise.
I am also a hopeless romantic.

Many may find this contradictory. I find it perfectly natural. Good D/s, or Dominant and submissive, relationships are inherently romantic in nature.

> *As I write these words, my servant boy, H, is in the livingroom, polishing my leathers and boots while wearing a remote control electrical shock device strapped to the genitals. Of course I have the control switch, hanging from a cord, nestled in my cleavage. H is my full time submissive and I am, at all times, H's Queen. Our relationship is deeply steeped in leather romance.*

To the uninitiated eyes, the eyes of the general public, it's hard to understand the core truth of the warm, emotional nature of D/s. I don't blame them for their misconceptions. There are no reference points for the public to grasp and learn from the inner workings of such private relationships. What references do they have? The media? The act of erotic dominance and submission, as well as those who choose D/s as a full or part time life expression, are at best treated as titillating sexual game players and at worst depraved sub-humans. The purely visual eroticism of the movie version of *9 1/2 Weeks* is a great example of the former. The "Gimp" character in the movie *Pulp Fiction*, clad in a leather bondage suit and kept in a cage by abusive masters, is a prime example of the latter. (Although, his leather suit was awfully well made for poor rednecks who were his captors.) Like any marginalized group, the public attributes all aspects of social ills to D/s people. We're threatening freaks in the eyes of the genteel folk.

What do John and Jane Q. Public think of us D/s practitioners? They suspect that we are emotionally and physically crippled and dysfunctional. It's not an uncommon assumption that some childhood trauma has scarred us, making us incapable of loving in a sincere and respectful way, and such that we require the emotional barrier of kink to enjoy any affection. They may even suspect sexual dysfunction. Perhaps they think that we have internalized disrespect, misogyny and self-hatred. D/s, to them, cannot possibly fall within the realm of true love between fully actualized and equal people. They also think that we are not capable of affectionate long-term relationships and furtively go from one unfulfilling relationship to another. And don't forget we're sick and disgusting.

If you read the above paragraph again, it sounds just like what people used to say about gays and lesbians. (And some still say this about queer folks.) Hmmm… funny thing….

Why do they even waste the energy judging and criticizing private sexual practices? What's the perceived threat here? Commercial images seen in movies and other media exploit the biological, evolutionary and social validity of all forms of sexuality and create social repression around sexuality, all for the mighty rating and the dollar. This, in turn, feeds popular condemnation of "deviant" behavior. I suspect that this sort of social rejection may be a manifestation of people's fear of their own uncertain desires. Most of us have some element of fluidity in our erotic mental landscape. But for someone who is rigidly attached to their sexuality as proof of the way the world should work, the admission of fluidity when it comes to their fantasy and arousal might spell the downfall of civilization as we know it. As the Bard put it, "methinks the lady doth protest too much."

H is now kneeling on the floor next to me, presenting me a cup of tea. Did I force her to do this? No. Does it please me to see H's devotion to me? Yes. Does my submissive take satisfaction in a job well done? Yes. Does this simple act devotion and affection strengthen our relationship? Most certainly.

It's not to say that there aren't damaged souls among D/s folks. Plenty of people in all segments of the population are the emotional walking wounded. To say, however, that D/s is indicative of dysfunction in a person and in people's relationship is ludicrous as saying that having brown eyes is indicative of dysfunction. To love is, simply, to love.

D/s relationships are very often misunderstood, sometimes even within the various enclaves of the kink/leather community. It's easy to explain the joys of bondage. It's liberating for a bottom to be bound so well that they can relax their body totally. It can be comforting to be embraced by the attentive efforts of the top. Even the more physically intense and visually intimidating scenes of pain can be relatively easily explained through the physiology of endorphins. Masochism is often compared to other physically intense pleasure activities, such as running the Boston Marathon. D/s, however, is not so easily explained by body chemistry or physical pleasure. After all, the skeptics would say, what's so erotically motivating and sexually hot about being bossed around?

The problem here is perspective. Vanilla eyes see an action and process it through the filters of their own experience. They simply interpret the action based on their subconscious analysis of the surface structure.

> *H's fingers are stained with shoe polish. It warms my heart to see that... the stains signify how much H cares for me.*

The superficial structure of the relationship appears to be built on inequality. The observer assumes that this superficial structure reflects the deep and underlying structure of the relationship. Thus the vision of a man on his knees before a woman holding a crop would be interpreted as signifying the core truth of the man's powerlessness and the woman's contempt for him. The observer has leaped to a value judgment. The truth in this picture is probably completely opposite of the observer's supposition.

All this explains the origins of prejudice and misunderstanding against D/s. This still doesn't explain the inherent romanticism of D/s relationships.

What's romance or romantic love, anyway? It's that intangible state that is so hard to describe. But we certainly can agree that it's a matter of the heart. Scholars say that romance is a long medieval narrative telling of the adventures of chivalrous heroes. That romance is a quality suggesting adventure and idealized exploits and an inclination towards the adventurous. A dictionary tells me that romance is "a strong, usually short-lived attachment or enthusiasm... and to woo, a love affair." A friend tells me that it's about getting to know another person deeply, loving them and being in love with them. Another tells me it's the state of two people's energy and affection focused on the each other 100%. Yet another, who has obviously suffered a recent loss of love, tells me that romance is the elated state of the heart before it's broken.

The internal experience of romance seems to be a sense of emotional fullness. It's not that the person is incomplete without it. Being outside of a romantic love relationship does not mean that they are somehow incomplete. Rather, a romantic relationship increases the quality of life and joy within them exponentially. What is perceived as being romantic is often the symbolic manifestation of this internal experience rather than the actual internal experience. The exchange of tokens, such as flowers, is merely symbolic of the inner joy. Unfortunately many mistake the superficial action for presence of the internal experience.

Thus Valentines Day or anniversaries can be a point of bitter contention for many couples. If the internal experience is the primary concern, than any token of appreciation for the joy experienced should be substitutable for the flowers or chocolates. Therefore a gift of a personalized collar should be just as much an expression of romantic love as a dozen roses if the intent is to convey the joy that the submissive gives the dominant. It's not the flowers, but why they're giving the flowers (or collar, or piercing, or domination....). For full-time D/s relationships, the symbolism of their affection gets incorporated into daily lives, manifesting in the (hopefully) meaningful rituals of kneeling, kissing boots, collar wearing, and so forth.

The fundamental key to understanding a healthy D/s relationship is seeking the mindful and formalized elements of the interactions that people would otherwise pass thoughtlessly through in non-D/s relationships. First, the union is entered into and begun consciously with the explicit consent of both parties. There is a clearly delineated and agreed upon beginning. This may take the form of a formal collaring ceremony, exchange of written vows (called a contract) or verbal acknowledgement from each of their relational position to the other. I've seen enough non-D/s situations simply fall into existence by the eagerness of one party and the inertia of the other.

The formalized acknowledgement of the formation of a relationship is a declaration that an adventure is beginning, that both people have some sense of the experience they are about to enter. They are, in fact, stating that they are now the heroes or heroines of their own romantic epic.

> *I will always recall fondly one late autumn evening when H took me to an elegant restaurant, both of us dressed gracefully in attire echoing the grandeur of Hollywood in the 30's... and after the dessert wine H asked formally to make a commitment to me.*

As part of the conscious entry into the joint journey, boundaries and terms are also agreed upon. This formalizes the scope of the relationship. Where some D/s relationships can fail, causing heartache, is when a shift in personal needs or a need for boundaries to be renegotiated are not recognized or acted upon. I am as guilty of this as others. When regular emotional maintenance is built into the structure of the relationship, D/s relationships can last for years. My friend Gumby and his wife/Mistress have been together for twenty some years in a relationship based on these principles!

The relationship is entered into because there is desire. Desire begets desire, fueling the passion of each person for the other. This desire is not simple sexual craving or that of physical attraction. There is certainly fondness and affection, even love. But it's also more than that. It's a desire to know this particular person in an intimate way that is so much deeper in the heart than simple physical intimacy. A prospective submissive's desire may be based partly in the hope that a special trust can be built between them, where loss of the ego state and peaceful surrender may be possible. The dominant-to-be may partly desire a singular loyalty and emotional safety where they are free to explore their hidden erotic hungers.

35

We live in a society that commonly confuses equality of people with sameness of want between individuals, especially in the erotic arena. We are not created with the same desires. Some like to lead, others like to follow. When we deny this diversity of desire, we are being blind to human nature for the sake of socio-political idealism. If one finds satisfaction in being a good follower in an experiential adventure and another finds fulfillment in making that happen through good leadership, what we have is a blissful match.

D/s is much like a dance; much like tango. Both individuals, well practiced in the art, know the fundamental steps and the elements that compose the dance. They approach each other in a formal formation, stop to recognize each other and begin the dance. One must be an exceptional lead; the other, an elegant follower. The lead's skill is pointless without the presence and grace of the follower: Fred would not be so great without Ginger. Although the components of the dance and even the music may be known, each dance is different as the lead steps into the follower's stance, and the follower responds in yet another different steps. What a beautiful dance is created this way! A unique dance imbued with energy, passion and intent is much like hot D/s play.

> *The lead and the follower in constant motion to the passionate music... Music of the forbidden underground. The sexual charge is so strong the voltage fills the air. The lead wills the follower to move and the follower resists just ever so subtly and then gracefully slides back yielding to the lead's will. Slow, Slow, Quick. soft, soft, Hard. Two equal human beings willingly step into roles of unequal power. Bodies swirl closely and yet never collide. The graceful lead plans steps ahead, yet never reveals but for the next step... The willing follower lets go of anticipation and lives in each step. They breathe in unison... Hearts beat faster... legs brush... pulses race... power ebbs and flows... passion rises....*

As in the tango analogy, good D/s does not diminish the equality and quality of either of the participants or their worth as human beings. In fact, it can be a great confidence builder for each individual and for the relationship as a whole.

Unfortunately today, this dance called relationship has become more like dancing at contemporary nightclubs where individuals go out and dance their own dance with another individual, each their own thing, hoping that they just might be on the same rhythm. Such a pairing may be destined to a vague sense of disconnectedness.

Good D/s relationships also manifest signs of the medieval romantic ideal of chivalry of honor, loyalty, bravery, courtesy and devotion. It's obvious that there is an expectation for the submissive to be loyal, courteous and devoted to the dominant. But the relationship is also based upon the loyalty, courtesy and devotion of the dominant for the submissive. The dominant must give the sub due respect, which means fundamental courtesy of a human being. She must be loyal to the relationship and committed to the care and protection of her submissive. This is a form of devotion to the union. It is also vital that the dominant honors the gift of surrender from the submissive. A submissive of quality would not be so foolish as to trust, much less surrender, to a so-called dominant who would not respect and honor their gift. Both people must honor the boundaries and vulnerabilities of the other. D/s has built into it a sense of mutual protectiveness and trust that flows both directions. D/s relationships are built upon respect and trust.

As I write these words, I gaze down with adoration to my boy, who in turns gazes back at me with a look of wonder and joy. Kneeling beside me in peace, no words spoken. None are needed. We know who we are to each other.

For many practitioners, a D/s relationship's formalized nature also brings a sense of domestic peace by consciously creating a space of order in a world filled with chaos and unpredictability. There is, for many, comfort in knowing exactly what their role in the relationship is and having the power to define it with awareness. In many non-D/s relationships, the roles of dominant and submissive parties exist, but they're not acknowledged at a conscious level or discussed as such. In such an environment where the roles become a set of default behavior, there is a great potential for quiet resentment and sense of dissatisfaction to build up.

H reminds me that there's something more to the richness of the D/s experience then what I've described so far. The boy is quite right. But here's my problem: how do I explain the emotional richness and pleasure in meaningful words to those who've never experienced it? How do you describe the pleasure of biting into a freshly picked, luscious sun ripened peach to someone who's only had hothouse fruits from Safeway? This quality of a special love is precisely what poets have been trying to put into words for thousands of years. After pages of attempting to write upon the romantic nature of the form of affection I practice called dominance and submission, I am still wanting for the words to convey to you the subtler nuances of it which I celebrate each day.

- Note: Time passes, relationships change. While the boy mentioned here, H, is no longer in service to me, I chose to keep these examples to honor the relationship and her time in service to me.

Ritual, Ceremony and Protocol in SM

It seems more and more folks in the kink scene are curious about the hows and whys of protocol and rituals in SM and D/s. At the many weekend kink events I attend, classes on various protocols, leather rituals and slave procedures are packed. Just a few years ago, among classes on basic bondage or flogging techniques, it was harder to find seminars on topics of rituals and procedures. Not so today: people are flocking to them. The same goes for classes purporting to teach 'Old Guard' protocols. I've observed on-line discussions and virtual diatribes on what the right way to properly collar a person is or how to correctly behave as a slave or master under various conditions. There's also some increase in people engaging in Gorean SM practices, based around social order and rules as delineated in a science fiction series, called *Chronicles of Gor*, by John Norman. Needless to say, I'm finding this whole trend very interesting.

The dichotomy is fascinating. Rituals and protocol, in a classical sense, connote an adherence to upholding precedents and rules, a commitment to conservation of value within a community. The desire for ritual and ceremony is an act of conservatism. Simultaneously, SM is deviant and outlaw sex. Let's face it: for all our politically correct spindoctoring of kinky sex, it is sex outside of the normative set, outside of the standard and accepted social practice. Many of us are drawn to kink because by the very nature of its taboo status and the power that such taboo brings with it.

Because of this taboo status, simplistic social arithmetic may lead critics to believe that SM would lead to sexual and social anarchy in individuals and groups. Yet that can't be any farther from the truth. The members of the various kink communities are drawn to and often bound by - for both good and bad - social conventions, rules and protocols. And we witness periodic surges of interest in rules and rituals of relationships and community within the perv set.

When it comes down to it, humans are tribal and social creatures in need of commonly identifiable and predictable behavior in order to function and survive in a constantly changing and unpredictable world. Protocols are social rules designed to automate sets of behaviors, reducing confusion and simplifying decision-making processes, allowing resources of time and energy to be expended on other variables at hand. It gives a sense of certainty of one's place in the world or community, or even within a paired relationship. Common rituals and protocols also create a sense of unity, bonding and meaningfulness of identity for the members.

Here's a concrete example: how to greet a person. If you are introduced to a business colleague at a professional conference, what do you do? You'd probably make direct eye contact, ask their name, say your name, and extend your hand. Your hand would in turn be shaken with a type and strength of grip considered appropriate for that person's station. But would you know what to do if you were in Japan, Zimbabwe, an Inuit village, Paris, Houston, Bernai or a maximum-security prison? The Dutch kiss three times on the cheek, the English twice, Californians once and the Japanese none. How do you greet them if the person is naked and having sex at the time? What if the person were collared and on her hands and knees, barking, at the time? If you had to worry about figuring all these things out on the spot, you wouldn't be able to get around to a simple conversation much less a good cruise for some future nookie with a new trick.

Protocols are sets of behaviors that make life easier by streamlining decision-making procedures. It is the formalized way in which diplomatic, religious and military communities recognize official and unofficial authority and hierarchy such that order and missions may be carried out most smoothly. It's also about having a set of good manners so that you assimilate well into a community, make friends, are accepted and validated. In the kink world the protocols may be as simple as "ask before touching another person's toys" or it could be complex as remembering how to properly serve a formal dinner party of dominants and submissives, while in semi restrictive bondage and with speaking restrictions. Protocols may eventually become a set of habitual behavior, like handshake or a soldier's salute, which require no particular deep thought. Like the salute, however, a protocol behavior may be executed in such a manner as to convey much more than habit. It may convey a person's respect or contempt. A handshake may reveal if the person likes you, finds you disgusting or just wants your vote. Protocols are subjective and arbitrary by nature, and may be defined by and apply to only two people, a small group of people or a larger community. I want my submissives to walk to my left and slightly behind, but you may have your slave walk to the right or directly behind. I decided on my protocol as a residue from my time in the US Army. You may want your slave to your right because you're left handed and you might smack her accidentally as you talk with your hand. None of this is wrong or absolute. It's only wrong if I assume that my set of protocols for my personal relationships are universal and your failure to know that is a personal affront or show of your ignorance.

Successful protocols I've witnessed and enjoyed in the kink community seem to have three basic elements in common:

- ***The Rule of Purpose in Protocol***
- ***The Rule of Grace in Protocol***
- ***The Rule of Economy of Motion in Protocol***

Perhaps we could call these the Rules of Protocol, and it maybe a good set of rules by which to sort out and create effective protocols in one's kink life.

A successful set of protocol serves the greater purpose and needs of the relationship and the community that the relationship functions within. A full time D/s relationship that's active within a Leather community in a specific region has a different purpose and needs that define their protocol than those you might find in a single-serving D/s scene for a couple of hours in the bedroom between people not active in the Leather community. In the former relationship, the protocol serves the relationship and the people. The people should never serve the protocol. In the latter situation, a set of protocols that consume the participants' focus simply for the fun of perfect execution may simply serve the over all goal of pleasure and momentary recreation.

The Rule of Purpose in Protocol

Let me be more concrete here. I've seen D/s scenes where the dominant required the submissive to learn about 50 or so different slave positions by name and number. Some were simple positions while others were quite elaborate in the sequence of execution with no apparent functional use. The submissive might execute each move with grace and economy of motion. But do the positions serve a purpose? If the game of precision is the central focus of fun for the scene, then fantastic! Much pleasure may be taken from these positions for both parties. The protocol may be used for other purposes too: the dominant may be using the exercise not for the usefulness of the positions themselves but as an intermediary tool to teach other lessons, such as voice recognition, swiftness, mental organization, erotic objectification, learning to function around physical dyslexia, etc. On the other hand, having so many positions to memorize and assume would hinder the smooth and daily functioning of full time service people. Is the effectiveness and speed of cleaning of my home somehow compromised due to overly restrictive and unnecessary position protocols? Then the set of behavior fails against the Rule of Purpose in Protocol.

The Rule of Grace of Protocol

Protocols have also been used as a tool of pride and exhibition. There is a polite limit to this. Dominants of quality are proud of their servants, slaves or submissives and often enjoy their graceful execution of protocol behavior. There is a point, however, when pride and pleasure cross the line to obnoxious showing-off. If a dominant's demand for the execution of the 57 slave positions get in the way of other people's social comfort, or if it's used as a tool to flaunt their " true dominance," then the protocol fails as it abuses the Rule of Purpose in Protocol. It's also no longer a socially elegant behavior, and so contradicts the Rule of Grace of Protocol.

Some protocols may also serve the greater purpose of a community. A good example would be the hanky code system developed by and imported from the gay men's leather community. What color of pocket handkerchief you wear and what side you wear it on expresses your current top/bottom status and activities you enjoy - or hope to enjoy later that night.

The Rule of Economy of Motion in Protocol

The Rule of Economy of Motion in Protocol is simple to grasp. It is executed fluidly with the minimum of wasted motion, and, perhaps, even with minimum extraneous thought. This is where practice comes in.

We've been discussing protocols in terms of bottom behavior, but protocol isn't only for the bottom, submissive or slave. Protocol applies to dominants and tops as well. A dominant who disregards his or her accountability to protocols established in the relationship or community will soon lose the respect of others. A tyrant, in the end, is alone, ruling over none and having control over none - especially of himself.

Ceremony

A *ceremony*, unlike protocol, is less frequently engaged in, compared to the on-going and constant execution of protocol behavior. A ceremony is a set of activities that serves to acknowledge a change, a demarcation of eras, both great and small. Weddings, graduations and bris are ceremonies. Birthday parties and bachelor parties are ceremonies. They may not be as formal as a wedding but they are social events that bring people together to acknowledge or celebrate a change. Ownership brandings, collaring or uncollaring rites are ceremonies. There is something different in a relationship's state of existence after the activities of a ceremony. A ceremony maybe public, private or even solitary; consider Romeo and Juliet's wedding versus Princess Diana and Prince Charles' wedding.

Most often the behaviors and actions within a ceremony are activities not common to daily life. They're special. You don't always get to wear a white ball gown, you don't always have your foreskin cut off, you don't always have to blow out a ton of lit candles on a cake. These activities are most often symbolically driven and may have very little practical purpose. I know very few people who consider candle wax covered cake as tasty or practical.

The people participating in a ceremony may have had direct influence in creating the ceremonial activities and deciding their symbolic relevance, such as a collaring ritual or a queer wedding. Sometimes the participants are simply adhering to what their predecessors did. The conventional wedding is a good example. In this situation the participants may or may not understand the origins of their own symbolic behavior.

The symbolic relevance or believed cause of the ceremonial activities may be completely different than what was originally intended. There are even times when the participants may have no idea of the historic relevance of the ceremony at the time. Consider the example of the baby during a bris. He has no clue what's going on, but with the action of the bris, his position within his world is clearly defined and that gives others in his community a point of reference. The others now know exactly what and who he is to them.

Like the bris, some ceremonies happen once and only once. Other ceremonies, however, may be periodic. New Years Day ceremonies in Japan or Christmas Mass in Vienna are good examples. Some D/s folks set a date to renew or reconsider their relationship or contract in a more formalized manner. Some ceremonies, such as weddings or collarings, may be intended as, or hoped to be, a once-in-a-lifetime event, though it just might happen again.

Ceremonies, much like protocols, are quite subjective and arbitrary, and may apply to and be recognized only by two people, a small group of people or a larger community. I may give a permanent collar of a necklace, you may weld a band around an ankle and another still will arrange to get matching tattoos. None of these are wrong or absolute. It's only wrong if I assume that my ceremonies for my personal relationships are somehow universally relevant.

Ceremonies are very meaningful to those involved. They may also be less practical in their apparent action than protocol while having a greater sense of grandeur and elaborateness. They may even be highly archaic, baroque or gothic in its ambiance.

Rituals

Rituals are a bit trickier to describe, but here I will attempt to share my own definition of rituals. Rituals, for me, fall somewhere between protocol and ceremonies. Rituals are less frequently engaged in than protocols, but are done more frequently than a ceremony. A ritual does not have to mark the change of personal, social or relational status but it may. Most often a ritual serves to remind or enforce a current status. Valentines Day observances serve to remind those in the relationship of the special bond. It may be more significant to the participants than saying "I love you" on a daily basis, because of the very nature of its formalized or fancy flourish, but it's still not quite as profound as saying "I do". It happens more frequently than a wedding but less frequently than a daily kiss. Rituals serve as punctuation over an otherwise potentially long period of time where the awareness of intent may be lost in routine. The ritual of a morning caning does not change the status of the relationship, nor does it have a particularly directly practical purpose, but it does serve to mindfully emphasize the status of the participants within the relationship and remind them of their commitments to their power dynamics. Rituals are subjective and arbitrary by nature, and once again, may apply to only two people, a small group of people or a larger community. I may have my sub kneel at the start of a scene, you may want your boots kissed and another still place a particular collar on their sub. And once again, none of these is wrong or absolute. It's only wrong if I assume that my rituals for my personal relationships are somehow universally relevant.

Yes, I repeated myself three times about the subjective nature of these activities. That was intentional. While some may find the subjectivity of protocol, ritual and ceremony obvious, it's not so for everyone. On one hand, I find my heart warmed by the individual kinkster's search for her own rituals and ceremonies. It tells me that kinksters are seeking meaning in their lives fully lived, relevance in their action and connections in their relationships and communities. Theirs are ceremonies that connect the person to person and also to previous generations of kinksters. On the other hand, some seekers of knowledge regarding rituals and protocols seem to be in search of some outside authority to hand them the proper rules to social survival or the guaranteed road map to spiritual fulfillment. Other pervs can give you ideas on what might work, but individual relationship and context determine action and relevance. As adult pervs we're given a spectacular opportunity to determine for ourselves our own customs. Why not take it?

What's curious, however, is why there's such an increase in interest in protocol at this point. I speculate that as our contemporary world offers us more and more choices for self-expression, sexual exploration and general social freedom, we find the vast choices paralyzing. This emotional paralysis leads many of us to turn to others so that they my hand us the right formula rather than to take a chance to figure it out for ourselves. Uncertain behavioral guidelines on top of the already precarious nature of deviant sexuality can make many of us feel unsettled. Given our culture of instant gratification and short attention span, we want the answers immediately, in a nice, neat pre-tested package. Unfortunately the matters of the heart and sex don't seem to ever work out into clean little pre-approved formulations.

The bad news is we have to figure it out for ourselves.
The good news is we have to figure it out for ourselves.

The Heart of Erotic Humiliation

One man crawls across the floor begging to lick his mistress's feet.
A woman is chided for her sexual appetite and is told to masturbate for her lover.
A grown man is dressed up as a baby girl and scolded for messing "her" dress.
These are all different aspects of erotic humiliation play.

I enjoy playing with humiliation.
    I don't' enjoy playing with humiliation.
Humiliation play turns me on.
    Humiliation play disturbs me.
I understand it.
    I am baffled by it.

You'd think that after all these years of playing I'd know this thing that I do inside and out. Well, I do and I don't. I can't be more honest than that. In my earlier days of SM play - and I was really just a kid then - I would enter a scene negotiation and clearly state that I would not engage in humiliation play. My initial rejection of the play was too adamant, too passionate to be dismissed as a simple lack of interest. Something in me was stirred by the play, in both good and bad ways, yet I was not able to sort out any of it. I lacked the insight and semantics to do so. Endlessly I would grill my friends, tops and bottoms, to try to come to some peace within myself, some comprehension of what in some aspects seemed like repulsive behavior. They would tire of my inquisition before I could ever get any sense of satisfaction.

Years passed. I set aside my troubled confusion and went on with my life. But the topic has since re-emerged into my life through various channels. Finally a nudge from the prorietrix of QSM (www.qualtiysm.com) to teach a class on the topic brought the subject back to center stage for me.

All this while I thought I was the one that was not getting it. As I researched, what emerged was the overwhelming prevalence of fascination and fantasy with erotic humiliation and a stunning paucity of relevant discussion on the nature of it. There are hundreds of porn books, stories and internet sites, yet even in the most respected SM information sources the discussion of the topic is at best brief. They all speak of the potential for psychological damage and the need for heavy negotiation prior to play. Yet none are able to tell me why it's such a turn-on. None are able to tell me why some aspects of erotic humiliation turn me on, but others do not.

So what is this thing called erotic humiliation play? Being a determined egghead, I set off once again to figure it out....

At the core of it, it's about eroticizing social discomfort or uncomfortable emotions such as shame, embarrassment, degradation or inadequacy. In order for this sort of discomfort to exist, there must be some internalized standard of behavior or a code of conduct, if you will. This code of conduct is based on socially defined sense of honor, prestige, self-esteem, reciprocity, and caste placement. We conduct ourselves in ways that we perceive to be appropriate behavior based on our place in the world, which is a delicate combination of external cues and internalized values.

When there's a discrepancy in one of these, we experience social discomfort leading to uncomfortable emotions. (While unable to find deeply thoughtful reading material in the community, I found seeds of inspiration for this essay in "Humiliation and Other Essays on Honor, Social Discomfort, and Violence" by William Ian Miller. Cornell University Press. © November 1993)

The social values that we have internalized contribute to our sense of self. The self, or the Ego, contains many values or beliefs of what it holds as true about itself. Let's call these the pillars of identity. Some of these pillars are more important than the others. It's like the walls and pillars of a house: some are load bearing, while others are ornamental, or create a socially expected division of space and function. These load bearing values, let's call the primary pillars, and the less important ones we'll call secondary pillars.

If a few of the secondary pillars of identity are off balance but the primary pillars are secure, and if this situation is in turn tied into a consented upon sensual situation, this may be conducive to erotically arousing humiliation play.

If, however, all or many of these pillars are disrupted by external forces, or if the primary pillars are fundamentally disregarded, then the play is no longer erotic and the experience becomes injurious to the person. This is a form of emotional abuse.

If we destabilize any pillars of identity, the resulting emotional discomfort actually creates changes in our physical system. Our pulse changes, neurotransmitters change their firing, the skin flushes and the breathing quickens. We know that fear and sex create this state of system arousal, and humans often find it exciting. That's why we enjoy scary movies, roller coasters, sports and sex. Kinksters often use elements of fear in sex play to keep things hot and exciting. We like to play with the effects of the Four F's: Fight, Flight, Feed and Fuck. While less obvious than fear, humiliation play can take the same course. The arousal created in the physical system by challenging someone's values and identity and the resulting uncomfortable emotions, the central aspect of erotic humiliation play, can be just as exhilarating for some. When this arousal is created by a caring partner combined with hot kinky sex, bingo! We have a successful erotic humiliation scene.

Let me try to explain this in plain English.

Jane believes herself to be intelligent, attractive, compassionate, friendly, honest, and fair. She also considers herself a "nice girl" and has grown up, to a certain extent, internalizing many of the sexual codes of conduct for "nice girls" including the values of sexual modesty and chastity. These are her pillars of identity. Of these, she holds in highest regard and as central to her identity, intelligence, attractiveness and compassion. These are her primary pillars, and while the others are also important to her, they are her secondary pillars. Let's say that she erotically submits to someone who considers her beautiful and

49

brilliant, but teases her in scene about being caught in a white lie about her sexual fantasies and for enjoying a lot of sex. He might say "You clever little slut! You told me that didn't turn you on!" In this example her secondary pillars, honesty and sexual modesty, are being challenged and her primary pillars, attractiveness and intelligence, are actually being reinforced. When combined with affection, encouraging tone and attitude as well as sensuality, this form of teasing and humiliation play can create uncomfortable emotions that may be extremely erotic to her.

On the other hand, if her dominant decided to chide her as stupid, ugly and self centered, her primary pillars of identity are torn down, leaving no solid ground of emotional safety for her Ego to stand upon, making the situation a threatening one to her core self. This is not erotic and can potentially damage the relationship or Jane's emotional wellbeing. This is abusive.

Let us consider the situation where Jane is the dominant in the SM scene. She still holds the same primary and secondary pillars of identity to be true. Let's say that she creates a scene where the bottom is treated as a dog for effects of erotic humiliation and the bottom enjoys this sort of play. She may feel her sense of fairness and equality in interpersonal relationships challenged and thus one of her secondary pillars is destabilized. During the scene, however, she is acting as the firm, strict yet loving dog trainer with creative training methods, so her primary pillars of intelligence and compassion are fortified. The enthusiasm and affection shown by her lover, now the "dog," also serves to reinforce and validate her as attractive to him. This helps to build an erotic experience for her and certainly for the bottom whom not only takes pleasure in the activity itself but also in seeing his top happy.

At this point you may be wondering if there's a list of activities to choose from that are considered definitely humiliating or erotically embarrassing for a scene. There isn't. Sorry. This is one of the problems as to why erotic humiliation play is so hard to explain. You can see what floggings or spankings look like and it's pretty easy to show someone the good and bad place to strike. Scenes that play with emotions or with the emotional interpretations of an action are necessarily subjective. Take for instance the action of kneeling before someone - a simple action, to be sure. But can you always know for certain its emotional relevance with respect to primary and secondary pillars? For one person it may be a sweet place of calm and sense of belonging. There's no dissonance of values and identity. For another, however, it may conflict directly with their sense of power and pride, creating a whole set of uncomfortable emotions. Now the question is, does the action or scene shake the primary or non-primary pillars?

While there's no clear list of what activities make for effective humiliation, I can give a suggestion: a scene that combines the psychological and physical will be far more effective then a scene that relies primarily on the psychological. For example, to sweetly chide a person for being a "little slut" with words alone may be moderately effective. But if the same words are used along with the bottom's skirt pulled up or during a play-acted "gynecological exam" will create a greater sense of erotic humiliation. When both the body and the mind are involved in the scene, the person is brought into the here-and-now and is more likely to experience the pleasures full strength, rather then engaging in well practiced distancing or emotional protection tactics.

This is all fine and dandy, but what is it that people get out of erotic humiliation play? There are as many reasons as there are players. Some major categories, however, do seem to emerge.

Humiliation play can function as the ritualization or emphasizing of power disparity of the roles taken by the players. Erotic humiliation can establish, enforce or emphasize power differential. In some cases, the humiliation in itself may not be erotic, but it serves as a means to an erotic end; D/s and the ability of one person to sensually strip power from another. For another, acting out the social taboo in itself may be the naughty pleasure. For some, they want to enjoy socially taboo activities, yet may still find that desire itself difficult to process. For instance, a man may want to wear women's panties but feel conflicted, so he needs another to push him over his own inhibition just for that moment. Here the bottom is in effect absolved of his desire as the symbolic responsibility lies with the top as she "made him" wear the panties, even though both parties know that's what he really wanted.

In other cases the top may use humiliation as a very effective tool for behavioral correction in D/s scenes. Humiliation play may be used for the bottom to prove their devotion to the top. Another may find being objectified a temporary relief from being a responsible adult in this world. Acting as someone's chair implies a very limited and clear set of duties. On top of that, no one else is being ignored in the same attentive way that this particular chair is being ignored by the dominant sitting atop it. Some enjoy it simply because getting away with being naughty is fun for its own sake. I have also known bottoms to experience insults as a form of reclamation of the self. One woman who, in her childhood endured non-consensual taunts on being overweight, now finds consensual humiliation scenes around her body shape reduces the power that the insults have over her. She's come to "celebrate her glorious and voluptuous fatness." And yes, these were her very words. When you think about it, how different is it then shifting the damningly negative power of the word "slut' held a half a century ago to how the same word is used with pride among non-monogamous sexual hedonists today?

Some may seek temporary distraction from worldly woes, allowing them the pleasure of being in the here-and-now, focusing strictly on their lover. People who go this route may be in search of some emotional calm and transcendence in a humbled and submissive state. I sense that some feel a tinge of unfulfilled desire after each scene as they seek to reach some unattainable state. This sense that there is something still greater just beyond the next turn may indeed be the state they seek; whether this is constructive or not depends on the person's relationship to humiliation play. Also, in the range of more spiritual quests, some find that humiliation provides temporary absolution for some perceived crime committed or redemption through symbolic mortification. Humiliation play may also allow a person to appreciate the mundane in a new way. (The pleasure of the opposable digit may seem once again remarkable after a persona has not been allowed to use their hands for the duration of a puppy scene.)

Some players find great intimacy in erotic humiliation play through shared vulnerabilities. The bottom gives the gift of deep personal vulnerability and the good top recognizes it as such. And for some, it's as simple as recognizing that humiliation play gets them hard or wet: a simple matter of sexual arousal.

This is a complex topic with great potential for pleasure, personal insight and exploration. Personally, I intend to keep investigating.... very diligently, of course!

The Essential Dominant – Notes from the Dungeon

What makes for a dominant of quality? In a flood of information circulating in publications, media and the net, sometimes the young dominant may feel a bit overwhelmed. It's easy to lose sight of the basics in a frenzy of information gathering. Over several installments we'll discuss some of the fundamentals on how to polish one's dominance towards a more fulfilling sense of self and greater adventures. This was originally written with sisterly sharing in mind, so you'll find that I'm a using "she" rather than "he." While I'll be using the feminine pronouns, please understand that most of what we discuss will be common across gender and certainly across orientation. So, gentle readers, please consider "she/he" and "domme/dom" to be interchangeable.

From the Core

Effective dominance comes from the core of the person.

No amount of fetish wear or powerful looking garments can make a domme out of a woman who hasn't worked on her power and grace within. Having a collection of great toys won't make you a great domme either, it just means that you know where to shop. It doesn't mean that you know how to use the tools to create the desired effect that pleases you the most. The same goes for skills. Knowing a lot of techniques alone does not make you a great domme. It'll make you a decent top, but that's different than being a dominant. You might be a good service top, a lovely submissive sadist, or a fine egalitarian sadist, but these are different – though no less valid – than being a dominant.

Conversely, you can be dressed in nothing more than ordinary, daily clothing, using no equipment and displaying no particular flashy techniques, and still demonstrate deep and powerful dominance.

Let's talk about some of the basic core strengths of the good dominant...

- Know the domain of your influence.

A good domme always understands when dominant behavior is appropriate. She knows when to go into domme headspace and when to turn it off. She knows that she is not in a D/s relationship with the entire world. She knows that the tone and attitude of dominance wielded upon unconsenting people around her will only earn her their contempt and disrespect. She knows that such behavior is displayed only by the misguided, insecure and bullying. She doesn't condescend to business people she has dealings with: she treats them with kindness. She doesn't assume strangers will bow to her powers: she treats them with the respect that all humans deserve. She doesn't let the dominant energy bleed into an egalitarian relationship once a hot scene has ended. If she is in a D/s (Dominant / submissive) or M/s (Master/slave) relationship, she understands that her dominance may be expressed differently even within that single relationship. What she does in the bedroom or dungeon with her slave will be quite different than what she would do at the slave's workplace, wouldn't it?

- Confidence is the root of power.

A good domme understands that the ultimate aphrodisiac for the sub is the dominant's genuine self-confidence. Sometimes it may come off as cockiness, but the difference between the cocky and the self-confident is the source of validation. The cocky dominant needs to see her greatness reflected in the eyes of others, while the confidant dominant simply knows what her powers are. The good domme has taken inventory of and is comfortable with her own talents, skills, assets and strengths. She is confident enough to see her own flaws clearly.

- If a dominant cracks a whip in the woods and there are no submissives is she still a domme?

Absolutely! A good domme is not defined by the other, in this case the presence of a submissive, but rather she is defined by a sense of self and comfort in her own identity as an erotically dominant woman. She knows that it is false confidence to need to define herself by the others around her. Every dominant from time to time will find herself alone, whether by circumstance or by choice. She knows that her relationship status does not change who she is fundamentally.

- Seduce... Don't force

The good dominant knows that the ultimate power is that of persuasion. To get the submissive or bottom to want to do for you what you command of them - that's dominance. Any fool with a fearsome enough weapon can force another against his will to do things. That's the power of the brutish, fearful people and those lacking in self-confidence. It's downright annoying! The art is in bringing out a desire previously unaroused in the submissive thanks to the domme's persuasive powers, confidence and graceful seduction.

As one of my favorite leather teachers, Joseph Bean, loves to say... The number one job of the dominant is to continually seduce consent from the bottom.

- Humility begets respect

The good domme understands that she must be humble in the presence of the magic that she invokes: that magic of wondrous connection created in the arena of genuine D/s. There is a moment, during the most amazing scenes, where the rest of the world melts away, leaving a universe of two, the domme and the sub. In a universe of two, she is god, for that brief moment and in that time warped space. To accept that, she must be humble. She must know that she is but a mortal woman at all other times.

Such humility has the amazing effect of creating a calm aura, bringing an air of grace and elegance that is deeply alluring. This sincere humility and consequent grace earns a domme the quiet respect from others around her and most certainly of her submissive.

Without respect, there is no leadership. Without leadership, there is no dominance, only brutish domineering.

- To get your partner's submission, give them respect and gratitude.

The good domme knows the value of giving respect and thanks to well-executed submission and service well executed. Even the cool and aloof have their ways of showing respect and thanks. The good domme respects the humanity of the submissive even after the most intense objectification scene. She is thankful for the act of submission given, even when it may appear externally as if it were wrenched from the submissive. She knows that, in the end, it is the submissive who chooses surrender. She knows how difficult true surrender is and is in awe of that. She knows that it takes the truly strong and self-aware to fully submit and she appropriately shows gratitude for that.

The good domme knows that the limits and emotional vulnerabilities of others must be respected. That includes respecting the limits of a non-participating parties to not have to deal with wantonly splattered dominant attitude. It includes respecting the limits placed by the submissive, for such consideration on the domme's part leads the submissive in feeling truly safe with her. Such a sense of safety often leads to deeper surrender.

As a dear friend of mine, David V, said: "Always be respectful in spirit, even if the scene is not."

- Be honest in these things: your desires, your limits, your flaws and your errors.

The good domme knows clearly what she enjoys in kink play. If she doesn't she'll simply be pushed this way and that by the desires and projected expectations that others have of her. Like a leaf pushed around in the currents of a fast river, she will always be haunted by a vague sense of helplessness and lack of control. What's a dominant if she doesn't have control over her own pleasure?

The good domme knows her limits and displeasures just as well as her thrills. The art of the polished domme is in setting boundaries gracefully in such a way that that the submissive wants to respect her.

She also knows where her flaws and weaknesses are and simply accepts them. She is strong enough to know that covering up with bravado and pretending her flaws don't exist is a sad shell game played by the insecure domme. She is, after all, comfortable in her humanity. She also knows where her technical limitations are and knows how to work around them to avoid undue risk. She knows when to seek more learning to increase her skills, and does so without making each step of dominance education a battle of egos.

When she makes an error, which she knows must happen from time to time, she sees the error she has made and acknowledges it. Then she does what needs to be done to correct the situation, checks with the sub and moves on. She neither overreacts nor ignores the errors.

- *Decisiveness is enthralling.*

The good domme knows to approach dominance with decisiveness. Each action is committed with mindfulness, whether arrived at by conscious thought and decision or by instinct. The person who openly waffles in the act appears to have no control – even over even her own thought. It is fine to wonder and consider choices in one's mind. It is even fine to seek counsel and advice. Do that with decisiveness as well.

The good domme knows that with decisiveness comes the potential for her making the less than optimal choices. This is simply being aware of consequences. She takes responsibility for her actions and, once again with decisiveness, grace and compassion, handles those consequences.

My dear readers,
This brings to conclusion this installment of "The Essential Dominant: Notes from the Dungeon". Perhaps you have a question on the foundations of being the best domme of your own potential. Please send me questions and I'll enjoy the opportunity to address them. Just post your question to my on-line student and readers' lounge at http://groups.yahoo.com/group/divamidori/ or send me a letter to my post office box.

P. S.   *A personal pet peeve aired...*

     I've noticed a rather odd phenomenon in the last few years. I'm finding that people from some communities are pronouncing the word "domme" with the final vowel pronounced, as if they are saying "dommay." The final "e" is silent, as in "blonde" and "femme." This new-fangled pronunciation doesn't make sense to many of us in the kink community and does grate on the ears.

     I can't decide if it's worse than saying "subbie" which to me, and many submissives I respect, sounds rather diminutive, diminishing and insulting as an address for a seasoned submissive.

The Sexual Turn-on of Objectifying Women

She's bound to the black leather-topped table, her face and humanity obliterated by the smooth contours of a leather mask. I tear at her vulnerable flesh with implements of intense passions. A moment ago, she was my dear companion and equal. Now she is meat. My meat.

She is arching her back with strained grace through space defined by my web of ropes. I move her limb, just so, to accentuate the arc to please my aesthetics. She is beautiful. I make her comfortable. I am aware that I do this, not for her pleasure, but so that she may last longer and be more pliable as the means for me to express my erotic vision. A moment ago, she was my dearest consort and a fully complex human being. Now she is a raw canvas. My canvas.

I had a sexual secret. It's not a secret anymore. It's a desire that I now know to present cautiously to others, because it's still very taboo. I am often turned-on by objectifying my partners. I like to objectify both women and men. But right now, my turn-on by the objectification of women is foremost on my mind. If I were younger, I'd feel more than a twinge of guilt as I admitted to this. I don't feel that so much now. The discomfort in my own emotion has faded to a curiosity. I do, however, take pleasure in witnessing the uncomfortable squirming of others as I utter this truth that is part of my sexuality. I know they are squirming because they've felt what I've described, and they aren't comfortable with it in themselves to admit, boldfaced, to such desires.

It's pretty easy to explain why flogging, bondage and even heavier play such as piercings are such turn-ons. We blame it on the neural chemicals and other physiological effects. It seems biologically accountable, and this makes us feel comfortable. We find justification of sexual acts in theories about the organic predetermination of pleasure. Nonphysical taboos, such as sexual arousal from the objectification of others or from being objectified, still make us nervous, because we can't explain them away. It's still politically incorrect, even within the SM / Leather / Fetish community, to acknowledge that we enjoy stripping away the humanity from a person for pleasure and play.

It is even more socially incorrect, causing some serious discomfort in people, when the objectification is of a woman, and worse still, by another woman. If I'm really a feminist as I claim to be, how could I do such a thing to another woman? Mustn't I always respect another woman and cherish her complexity? Isn't my desire and action an outward expression of some internalized self-loathing and misogyny? Do I have some sort of God complex?

> Answers respectively:
> With glee.
> No, not if the two of us don't want to.
> No.
> Yes, in some ways, yes.

> Allow me to explain.
> Sex is one of the few arenas left to us "civilized" citizens of "First World" nations where we are permitted to indulge in the performance of primal drives. We are allowed a slim portion of our existence in sex, to play out the fundamental human psychological dramas. Sports are the other sanctuary for expressing the profound honesty of our raw selves. In both worlds, we are permitted to show our teeth of aggression and bellies of subordination. We spit, hiss, growl, compete, moan, touch, embrace, shudder, cry and scream. We long to belong, we hunger to conquer and we are inexplicably driven to create beauty. We are all quite complex creatures with multilayered needs and desires, many of which are at times at odds with each other.

I want to be respected for my complexity, yet I wish to be adored for some singular aspect of myself. I wish for a full and busy life, yet I crave simplicity and focus. I want to share in the responsibility of pleasure, yet I want to just "get done" free of effort. I wish to honor equality, yet I feel a need for power and hierarchy. All these things apply to sex as well.

This is simply to illustrate that we are conflicted and complex creatures. If I am to be self actualized as a woman and a feminist, I must own the conflicted nature of the self and claim my sexual pleasure, complexity and all. To do that, I must be open to all my own social discomforts that my lusts bring forth. Then I must find another person whose desires and complexity dovetail with mine. If I wish to conquer to get off, then I must find another who gets off by being conquered. The matter of force then retreats into the sanctioned arena of consensual sexuality.

There is a huge difference between the erotic objectification we're discussing and the everyday objectification of women by the world. That hurts. It hurts because women did not consent to or set up the situation. It hurts because the people objectifying her do not see the complexity and richness of who she is. Instead of starting from a place of compassion, love and understanding, which is narrowed down to the simplicity of symbols, it is a brute force refusal of humanity with no room for seeing the whole person. It is a weapon used to attack others in order to protect the fragile offender. Instead of celebrating complexity, it comes from the fear of complexity.

But why the objectification of other women? There's an inkling, deep inside me, that perhaps I seek this companionship in another woman because she might understand my needs better. Perhaps, in acting out the hunger to conquer, posses or create upon another's flesh, I seek to express my own counter-part desire in the other woman, thus creating a fully balanced sphere of desire. Somewhere I become both her and I. The orgasm leaves me calmed, not simply because a physical need has been sated, but because I have created a moment of balance and harmony within my own complexity.

Then perhaps the dirty truth is that I am both the top and the bottom for a moment. I am creating a universe of two people where I determine the actions of both and my desire permeates both. I become, for a brief and fluttering instant, omniscient. Then, for that one moment, in that small universe, am I not a god? I create a simplified and pure world reduced to lust and symbols. As a god, I have nothing else to

61

worry about except to fulfill my desires. As part of god, she has nothing else to worry about except to surrender all worries.

Is this escapist? Yes, it is. But that's what pleasure and entertainment is about, isn't it? Sex and sports are, in the end, about pleasure and entertainment. When we have arenas within which we can focus on creating pleasure, play with our primal drives, and forget our obligations, we feel freer. It's a mini-vacation from the additional complexity that the world thrusts upon us.

To give a few examples, my friend, AX, has a dirty little fantasy. She wants to be bound, blindfolded and used simply for her three holes by an unknown number of people. This isn't simply hot and nasty; it's mini-vacation that's freeing and self-celebratory. Objectifications take on many forms. Some people are the clay to the artist, others are the pure sexual victims for consenting perpetrators. Still others are transformed to pets or to furniture. Certain forms of Dominance/submissive and Master/slave relationships take on qualities of objectification as well.

Do you get off on consensual erotic objectification? As a feminist, as a woman who claims my sexuality as my own, and as a complex and very human person, I do.

Wrong Reasons to Do SM

Are you a kinkster? Are you a part of the SM community? Do you identify as a leather person? If you've answered yes so far, do you know why are you a member of this community? Has it fed your needs? Has it made you happier? Has it brought you more peace within yourself? Have you found intimacy and harmonious connections with people that you did not otherwise? If so, I congratulate you.... You have found a corner of the complex social network of humanity that's right for you.

If you've not found these things, perhaps, just perhaps, you might be seeking to quench your thirst in the wrong watering hole. You may be seeking your bliss on the wrong pilgrimage.

Recently I've encountered a few situations where I've wondered if a person's need to belong to the kink community was positive or healthy. I'm not talking about the rare egregious nut case murderers who prey on on-line BDSM players and stuff them into 55-gallon drums. I'm talking about everyday people who find themselves in search of something within the leather world and constantly feel unhappy or unfulfilled. I have met such people in casual conversations at leather events, as submissive applicants, as tutorial students and even in my circles of friends.

There's a person who thought that being a house boy/servant/ sex slave would be a great way to get laid and have a comfortable place to live. There's another who uses the premise of TPE (Total Power Exchange) to deprive his sub from having contact with her friends and family. I know of a person who doesn't like any SM play but wanted the seeming tenderness of after-care, so would put up with acts that were uncomfortable to him. There are bottoms who, with artful passive aggressiveness, guilt-trip their tops into serving their needs. There are those who believe that D/s justifies their broken self-image, who feel themselves worthless in the absence of another, and who have deep self-esteem issues – tops and bottoms both. I know of dominants who force their boys and girls into high-risk sex in the name of obedience.

Why so much of this lately?

During the past several years there's been a great effort to give positive PR to the SM life. That's fine. I'm all for reducing the stigma against alternative sexual practices between consenting adults. But in the rush to show the joy of kink, perhaps we've done too good of a job. Perhaps we've made the leather life seem an Eden of sexual adventurousness and a panacea for personal and erotic problems. We've also put stock in our reputation as a community that welcomes all adults with open arms, regardless of their proclivities, perversions or dysfunctions. We talk about the joys, the physical highs, the spiritual paths, the honored commitments, the deep bonds, the tenderness, the primal joys, the enlightened communication... Sounds wonderful, doesn't it? The spin job by the enthusiastic disciples of perviness has done its work... in some quarters. (Although not anywhere near enough in the realms of legal defense, employment protection, and mental health diagnoses.) Understandably, this is what enthusiasts do. I'm guilty as charged. We are thrilled and delighted and only wish to be understood. With such wonderful earnest cheerleading, especially in the world of the Internet where no one can be held accountable for their words, people have been coming out of the woodwork to find SM munches, clubs, play parties and play mates.

What we, the believers haven't mentioned are the mundane details, the downsides, and the realities.

- o If you are broken, SM will not fix you.
- o Your dominant may play your mommy or daddy, but you're still an independent adult with adult responsibilities to the world.
- o Poor social skills cannot be disguised as dominance.
- o Poor social skills cannot be disguised as submission.
- o You can't get a date just because you bought a whip or a collar.

- Only you can make yourself worthless.
- Only you can choose to be powerful.
- Consensual slavery or D/s is not a meal ticket and a free room.
- Total Power Exchange isn't.
- Total Power Exchange can't protect you from a restraining order.
- Empty rituals will not lead to love.
- Controlling another's life doesn't mean that you have control over yours.
- Consent is a moment-to-moment experience and does not stand permanently.

Our community ideology states that SM isn't abuse and there's no place for abuse in good SM, but here's the reality... Abuse in our community happens and we don't always talk about it. It may be the abuse of others or the abuse of the self. I have no idea of what the incidence of abuse in the SM community might be. I have no idea as to whether it's greater, lesser or at par with the general population. But it's there.

Sometimes we aren't certain if an interaction between members of a couple is abusive or consensual behavior. When the dominant silences the sub, is that abuse or is it protocol acceptable in their household? We can't always tell from the outside of the relationship, whether the sub maintains agency of their life and consent or if a sense of powerlessness is pervasive to a point of Stockholm syndrome like helplessness and subjugation. We aren't always certain from the outside whether the domme is enjoying newfound sexual confidence or is actually a reluctant and domineered Wanda to another selfish Severin straight out of *Venus in Furs*.

Yes, many people start out in SM feeling uncertain... even insecure and lacking confidence. This is to be expected in any new adventure. I'm not talking about the uncertainly of entering a new world. I'm concerned about people who are broken and enter SM to put a leather outfit on and hide their cracks. Some people may believe that this is their only option or the only place they belong. Maybe the broken people mistake simple acceptance for true happiness and deep belonging.

You can't always know who the very broken people are. Sometimes we don't even recognize them when they're looking at us in the mirror. Many of the broken have fully internalized the wording of the dogma, catchphrase and slogans of the SM community. They sound great on paper... or in their Internet profile. They sound great during the interview or negotiation process.

Here's one thing to look for; does the SM or D/s they do really turn them on? Does it make them hard or wet? Do they have erotic fantasies about kink? Are they truly happier for being a part of the community?

Along with genuine arousal, are they able to empathize with other people? Do they have friends of quality? Do they have a sense of self worth and self esteem balanced with a healthy sense of humility and integrity? Are they able to interact properly within and outside of the SM community? Has it fed their needs? Has it made them happier? Has SM brought them more peace within the self? Have they found intimacy and harmonious connections with people by way of SM explorations?

In the end, there is no one that's accountable for us and our own desires but ourselves. Have you looked into your own reason for your life of kink and leather? Do you have agendas beyond that of honest pleasure? Are there hidden hungers or needs that you substitute with your kink enthusiasm? We ought to take a good look into our own hearts from time to time, to examine and monitor our own health and make sure that we're choosing SM for the right reasons. Nobody's going to do it for us – at least nobody without their own agenda.

25 Years: Kink State of the Union

Rest assured, oh fellow kinksters, there will always be pervs as long as humans have cerebral cortexes and libidos. War, disease and disaster only divert our attention for the moment. Then, we return to our obsessions with even greater vigor, all the more so for having tasted mortality and touched uncertainty. The existence of deviant sexuality in the population won't change.Elements of the kink life, however, have undergone some considerable changes in the last quarter century. Some are good and some are troublesome. Technology seems a major factor in both cases.

Twenty-five years ago I was just a little teen girl in Japan. A shy child, a bit too small for my age, I had no idea what my future held. I certainly didn't figure I'd be writing about sex. I didn't even read or write in English then. I was too sheltered to care about dating, much less sex, but I already possessed the knowledge of self-pleasure. My fetishes were yet to be expressed but the earliest signs were there. My sexuality churned and bubbled silently inside of me, waiting to be sprung upon the unsuspecting world.

The world I grew up in, over a quarter of a century past, seemed so much more innocent, both in Japan and in the States. I was not bombarded by images of sex. My pubescent and pre-pubescent body wasn't sexualized and commodified by the media. I did not have to worry about sexual predators, much. Computers belonged in huge corporations, not in my bedroom. In 1978 abortion had only been legal for 5 years in the States. The gay bathhouses thrived and no one had heard of the "gay cancer" or HIV. A cocktail was a drink, not a medication regimen. Speaking of AIDS, "We Are The Champions" by Queen topped the charts then; thirteen years later we would to lose Freddie Mercury to AIDS. "Coming Home" won at the Academy Awards. Does anyone remember that movie? "Debbie Does Dallas" was released, and we all remember *that* title. Carter was President of the USA. The first "Test Tube Baby" was born. The cloning of sheep and babies, fetal stem cell controversy and Viagra couldn't even be fathomed. George W. Bush ran unsuccessfully for Congress from West Texas. San Francisco supervisor Dan White assassinated Harvey Milk, the first openly gay official in the US. We couldn't imagine the US having gay congress members back then. We have them now. Mork & Mindy were the leading role models for alternative families, no Osbornes, no Will & Grace. Burt and Ernie were the gayest couple on TV, but they were seriously closeted.

The Society of Janus, founded by Cynthia Slater, was just 4 years old then, and is now one of the longest running SM organizations in the US. Later, Cynthia was one of the first female victims of AIDS. The next year, 1979, Tony DeBlas started Dungeon Master magazine, nearly inventing the kink technique how-to publishing track. A kinky couple named Kat and Layne in San Francisco started a sex rag called *The Spectator. Skin Two* magazine didn't even exist.

I can't personally speak about everything that happened in the past quarter century of pervery, but I can talk about what I've noticed in my 15 years of sexual and kink explorations, based out of SF and spanning a continent or two. As I look back I am of two minds. On one hand I am thrilled at our progress and hopeful for the future of sexual freedom and true individual liberty. On the other hand, I am discouraged to see the creeping conformity within and outside the kink community and some other troubling trends.

On the bright side, the Pandora's box of sexual information, once opened, can't be easily shut. In the United States, we have been fortunate enough not to suffer at the hands of extreme oppression and outright brutal assault to freedom of information on the part of authorities. (although Mr. Ashcroft and the Bush administration are trying to remedy that situation.) Sexual information and imagery, regardless of accuracy, is widely available. People are simply not as shocked by the presence of sexual variety today. Gays and lesbians on TV are now 'cute' and trendy main characters, no longer confined to the roles of freaky pedophile suspects or to the realm of tear jerker Hallmark melodramas about the one dimensional 'poor fag victim with a heart of gold who can't help it.' Fetish wear is da bomb for the Hip-Hop and just plain Hip set. Just remember that where Lesbian & Gay issues have gone, so may go other sexual minorities, such as bisexuals, transfolk and the pervs... but they must be just as media-savvy and politically strong to follow their more-experienced lavender brothers and sisters. But at least now the potential is there. Now the kinky know that they're not alone. We know that there are other kinksters and sexual minorities out there to band together with.

Apart from the politics, at a more personal level, individual kinksters now have their own consumer goods industry. Where in the past there was a smattering of stores and hidden manufacturers, now there's a whole free market eager to compete for your hard earned disposable income. In the past decade alone fetish clothing and equipment manufacturers as well as consumers have enjoyed an unprecedented growth in quality, quantity, availability and creativity. Technological improvements in manufacturing processes helped, but more importantly the capabilities of Internet commerce such as eBay, and fetish imagery in the general media, have helped to fuel this growth. Fetish and pervery have become an accessible, celebrity-endorsed glamour-taboo, just edgy enough to make the bearer hip. Preexisting design houses, such as Gucci, didn't miss the opportunity for increased visibility and marketing, and neither did newer designers, such as Alexander MacQueen, looking for a niche in which to flex their creative muscles. With the Internet, even small shops in remote places could show their quality work to an appreciative consumer market.

This same information technology also connects fellow pervs, locally and globally, with an immediacy hitherto unknown. Kinky parties, events and clubs are organized almost entirely by electronic medium now. Today, events happen faster, more frequently and in more places. E-networking has given rise to a new form of perv liberation activism and anti defamation work as we saw in the Spanner case in the UK and in the States spearheaded by the National Coalition for Sexual Freedom. Because of the anonymity of electronic media, it's less risky and stigmatized for people to get the scoop on the parties and the politics. Travel junkies like myself rely on the Net to keep in touch with friends from far-flung places and make new friends. E-mail has now replaced the old "letters of introduction" people used to need to get into clubs and closed SM societies. A whole new dating and mating ritual has arisen around internet culture, making it easier we erotic deviants to dramatically increase our chances of meeting compatible playmates.

Once you've found people to play with, how do you get to down to kinky sex? Today, more than ever, there are wonderful resources offered for the sexually curious. Previously people had scant materials, there were no how-to books and skills were passed from person to person in closed and secret community networks. Today classes and workshops are popping up all over the place. Less and less does sexual shame grip the throats of Middle America. The army of sexual knowledge-bearers led by such trailblazers as Betty Dodson, Good Vibrations, Carol Queen as well as maverick organizations such as TES, Janus, bring joy and improved sex skills to the boudoir. Just think of the sheer increase of orgasmic and even ejaculative women out there now, compared to 25 years ago. Secretive SM socials and furtive leather meetings have grown into multi-hotel affairs that have become major travel destinations and generators of local capital.

While ideally globalization and aggressive information spread can create exchange of ideas, creativity and individual expression, in actuality they also have the effect of blanding cultures and increasing uniformity in behavior and thought. Just think McDonalds and Starbucks. The forces of conformity are also creeping into the ranks of the sexually marginalized. Proper gays and lesbians want nothing to do with the radical fairies and leather folk. We embarrass our upstanding rainbow family with our 'socially inappropriate' activities and insistence to be recognized. We threaten their bid to be accepted among the sprawling middle class.

Even within the leather community, those who don't 'play by the rules' are looked down upon. As we flout the conventions of proper attire in society, we find ourselves looking like a bunch of leather clones in heart and in wardrobe. Where does this set of rules to conform to come from? You guessed it, by all the ways and means we disseminate information. Somewhere along the way a 'good idea' becomes 'the law.' Social conformity gives us a sense of comfortable validation without self-examination - an "Us" to belong to and a "Them" to shun. Some people conform, wanting desperately to belong, even if kink isn't their thing. There are those who wind up in the BDSM community, after exposure to it by the media and the Internet, because there they can find affection and admiration. They want that so badly that they will pay with their flesh, by pretending interest or by acquiring a skill to become popular. I'm talking about the folks who do it but aren't really into kink. It's sad.

There's another nasty little side effect to all these happy sex seminars and massive perv-o-palooza, too. The joy of sexual exploration

70

and self-discovery is suffering the rigor mortis of "Seminarization" of SM, especially in the States. Attending classes sometimes seems to be the criterion by which a person defines himself or herself as kinky. We need good information and quality education to maximize the fun, but there's a point where we can lose sight of the forest for the trees. The focus on technical expertise and sometimes near-paranoid focus on risk obliteration paralyzes players from living the joys of the experience itself. The beaurocratization of radical sex can foster a social climate of conformity and social hierarchy. This can't be a healthy way to encourage individuality. I should know, after all, I came from Japan, the land of conformity. Many leather events have become so unwieldy, large, bureaucratized and impersonal that I wonder if I've walked into a sexual festival or a convention of Home Depot enthusiasts run by the administrative arm of the Swiss Army. I have a suspicion that all this zealous organizing, teaching and perfecting serves to protect nervous kinksters from seeing the sexual animal in their own soul.

The conveniences of technology have other costs. The kink subculture, like the rest of society, has fallen victim to the information-age disease: technology-induced compression of time, patience and pleasure. As members of a culture now accustomed to communication with the depth and complexity of sound bites, we now seek fast and uncomplicated fulfillment of our pervy desires. Desperate for the rare commodity called time, people seek to meet their companions efficiently and move on with the 'action' and relationships as fast as possible. Kink courting is fast being reduced to the formulaic matching of preference checklists followed by a few e-mails before the initial meeting at a hyper-organized, clean and well-lit dungeon party.

I fear that flirting, teasing and building desire through shared passions, never mind dark alleys and seedy dungeons, may become archaic as the horse drawn carriage – romantic yet frustratingly slow in reaching the destination. People also seem to approach pervy skill acquisition with the same type of perfunctory impatience. No time to savor the basics: we must get better and flashier sooner. The skills may be acquired quickly but where's the heart, passion and experience? "The tyranny of the technician," is an apt and devastating phrase coined by Mr. Guy Baldwin, describing this focus on mechanics and the tendency to quickly judge others' leather hearts based on skills. This fast paced trek towards more scenes with more people with flashier skills may cost us the passion underlying pervery. Has the desire for immediate gratification stunted our sensuality? Fetish and kink by its very nature is about longing, desire and mystery.

There's also the saddening trend of "experience bagging." I see people come through the kink scene much like some provincial tourists on a 10-day/15-city bus trip. They have the list of things they must do, events to go to, toys to own. Does the doing of these things, the checking of these lists, validate their pervitude? Perhaps this is simply the exuberance of new discovery. Perhaps no one has told them that the magic is in the journey mindfully taken. I can only hope that finding gratification in slow seduction and wallowing in pleasure may become fashionable again.

If the 1960's and 70's Sexual Revolution was the tumultuous teenage years of American sexuality, than the early 21st Century may be our national entry into mid-life crisis. Having survived the break away from the formal and weary paternalistic generation in the Civil Rights Era, the discovery of free wheeling (and irresponsible) sexuality in the 60s and 70s, and the materialism and self-absorption of the 80s and 90s; we now find our national mood turning to the contemplation of mortality and the intangible comforts sometimes mislabeled as "spirituality." Worse still, we have come to fear our children as bringers of chaos, a new unfathomable species to be wooed by marketers and coddled by parents. It is the mid life crisis of a people. Oedipus is realizing that he's just like his old man.

SM and sex both contain an enormous potential to bring us moments of clarity, calm and universality. So can Yoga, meditation, Native American rituals, Paganism, Kabala and Tantra. In the name of spiritual quests we seek the same self-validation in SM as we do borrowing, often out of cultural context, from other traditions and faiths. But although they may bring an endorphin rush, a few nice ego strokes or some self-validation, sitting in Lotus position, flogging someone or performing a flesh hook suspension aren't the automatic key to nirvana.

Spiritual practices have been squeezed into neat little sanitized packages to be acquired in weekend workshops and practiced in efficient speed formats in an attempt to calm the frayed American nerve as we grasp for something resembling love and intimacy. Leather, SM and kinky sex too can be stripped of their core joy and used as superficial band-aids for the soul. In the course of feeling good about ourselves, perhaps we fail to see that our 'children' and the world around are restless and another revolution may be upon us... Whether we like it or not.

Part Two: Fundamentals of Kink II

Photo by Steve Diet Goedde

Trust, Vulnerability and SM/Ds Part 1

Trust… a word that figures heavily into most any discussion around SM, D/s and leathersex. We hear about it all the time, from the most fundamental of SM educational literature, to advanced workshops, or even in casual dungeon chatter. We know it when we see it… Right? Or do we? Let's think about this. We have some ideas about what trust means in every day life. Yet in the context of SM and D/s, trust appears and disappears in seemingly irrational situations, appearing to defy common logic.

Let's consider a few examples…

> *Jo and Jane are a committed couple. They have a child, careers, and a long and happily shared life. They are also SM players who enjoy an occasional dungeon play party. They used to play a great deal with each other, but that's not been the case the last few years. Each of them finds it easier to have great play with friends in the scene or people that they meet at SM events. They have even had moments of deep clarity and exhilaration with these casual acquaintances… yet, lately it's been difficult to find it with each other. If SM and surrender in D/s is about trust, then, is the fundamental trust of their relationship eroding? In all other aspects the relationship is strong, yet the desire for SM continues to bring to the foreground the questions of trust, worth and love. In their hearts they struggle with the contradiction, always feeling somewhat uneasy, and the question remains unresolved.*

Mike is a single guy. He dates extensively and is quite popular. He's not lacking for attention or sexual opportunities. Once in a while, though, he calls a professional dominant for an experience of deep submission. He comes away from this feeling great! He's never brought this up with his tricks, dates or long time lovers. He really feels like he can trust his dom through all the experiences. He's not quite sure why he feels this level of trust. After all, the dominant knows practically nothing of him except his nickname, and he selected this dom solely based on a hot looking ad in a local paper.

Meet Master X, who has a good reputation in the community and creates really nice scenes. He plays with lots of people who love to have single scenes with him. What he really wants, however, is a long-term committed submissive. He's tried a few, but none of the relationships worked out. He's read the books, followed advice and the rules of how it's supposed to be done. He just can't figure out why it's not working in the long term for him. He starts to wonder if the whole idea of 24/7 might be hogwash.

Then there's the sensible professional woman, a well educated submissive, who lives in a city and seems savvy to the common hazards of urban life and staying safe as a single gal. She meets a dominant on-line and one weekend travels alone across the country for a fantasy kidnapping and play scene with her virtual dom. Her friends knit their brows with anxiety. Surely nothing good could come of her taking this sudden leave of her senses and good judgment.

What's wrong with these people? The simplistic conclusion is that each of these individuals suffers some serious hidden emotional wound, crippling them from loving and trusting appropriate people in a healthy way. (To slap on the label of "unhealthy" is a quick way to dismiss or condemn unfamiliar behavior. Obviously this is a common tactic for greater society to deal with sexual minorities like kinksters and GLBT folks, but it's also relatively common within our subcultural groups as well.) None of these individuals are sick, emotionally handicapped or even unusual. In fact, these anecdotal cases are not about any specific individuals, but rather synthesized from very commonly heard situations.

The problem here is not with poor judgment on the part of these individuals, but the misplaced expectations around what trust means in various forms of relationships. Trust is not a singular and universal state of mind. There are many conditions and variables affecting the degree and nature of trust. Most often the consideration of these variables happen subconsciously, instinctively or habitually. It's not always a decision thought through consciously. For example, let's say that your dearest best friend is an accident prone, lousy driver who's constantly getting into little fender benders. The two of you plan to travel to Asia together. While you'd trust him with your life on the climbing trails of Himalayas, you're not about to give over the steering wheel in Hong Kong. You've made the decision out of habit, without deep concern about the implication of trust in your friendship. No one would accuse you of being conflicted about trusting your buddy. Rather, they would perfectly understand your sensible decision. In the long run, your ability to distinguish between how much you trust him as a friend versus as trusting him as the designated driver allows your friendship to grow and means you can have wonderful adventures together.

In the context of SM and Ds relationships, similar processes also occur, but the problem is that the variables are not always clear, distinct or simple, and they are generally emotionally stickier than the example above. At the most fundamental level, before engaging in a scene, a player must consider if a prospective playdate has the necessary skill proficiency for the type of play they are negotiating. Beyond a basic skills assessment, many other variables affect the interaction and degree of trust in SM: Will this person respect my limits? Do they mean the same thing that I'm talking about? How much are they going to push my boundaries? What do other people think of this person as a player? What will my friends think of me if I play with this person? Will this person think well of me even after I've shared my darker fantasies with them? Will this person keep my sense of self worth intact or diminish it? Will I feel better or worse after a scene? Will playing with this person affect our pre-existing relationship? Can I transcend our daily relationship roles and enjoy a fantasy with this person? Will my vulnerabilities be used against me in damaging ways? Is this person interested in me and our relationship or is this going to be an expression of an ego trip? Is this person really trying to hurt me physically or emotionally or is this intended as shared fun? What do I risk if this scene goes badly? And so many more questions...

The process of building trust contains, among other things, an assessment of calculated risk. Then, we must consider for what end, or desired results, does this trust exist? What are we seeking? What are we protecting, and what are we willing to lose in order to gain the desired result?

Let's consider Jo and Jane's situation. Due to their long-term relationships, many common questions that affect trust for a first time encounter are irrelevant. It is clear that they are genuinely concerned about the other's pleasure in play and that boundaries will be respected. They know each other's skill sets. There is no doubt that fundamental trust exists between them to love and share so much of life's joys and sorrows together. Yet, there's a problem in the arena of play. In an attempt to rekindle the spirit of play they took the common advice and set aside a special date – to make it like old times. The whole experience felt stilted and in the end it really wasn't effective.

While it's true that for many couples the greatest obstacle is the lack of available free and private time, often there's more that goes into the reduced amount of play in long-term relationships. At this juncture it's easy for the couple to engage in mutual blaming or silent resentment building, leading to even less play and intimacy. What might be helpful is to consider the situation, not in terms of who is to blame, but rather what they perceive is risked if play takes place. Remember that the key word here is "perceived" risk, which may or may not reflect the reality of the situation, but nonetheless, affects the decisions made by the participants.

What perceived risks are there in SM and D/s play for those in long-term relationships? A whole lot! If you're playing with a near stranger or a casual friend, of course you'd have to worry about physical safety and hopes of maximal pleasure, but in an established relationship you have so much more to lose. What is the perceived risk if a scene goes badly? The entire relationship and the participants' sense of self may be on the line. This may sound dramatic, but it can be very true for many couples. When you first play with someone or you're first dating, you are certainly risking the possibility of losing the opportunity for greater erotic satisfaction, bruising your ego and wasting the time invested in courting. But the people's core values and sense of self worth are generally insulated from major injury. The cut can only be skin deep, so to speak. When lives become intertwined, however, more of the self goes on the line. Greater intimacy means greater exposure of one's vulnerabilities. A perceived rejection or judgment or a bad experience can impact the sense of self worth more profoundly. It can be a deep blow to the heart. This very nature of the deep intimacy of a long-term relationship can also lend to the hesitation of certain risk-taking behavior around sexual expression. Getting off at the risk of losing the relationship as it stands becomes less and less desirable as the value of the relationship increases. This tip in the scale stays in place unless there is a significant assurance that sexual adventurousness will not cost the relationship, or better yet, it presents a potential for significant improvement in the strength of the union.

Thus the perceived risk of adverse effects on the long-term relationship causes hesitation in play that might not be experienced in a casual play relationship. So it's easier for Jo and Jane to play with others. Unfortunately their mutual hesitation to play together may be seen to both of them as a display of loss of trust.

Ouch.

On a day to day level, the artifacts of familiarity might make it difficult for people like Jo and Jane to successfully suspend disbelief, to step out of the everyday, to enjoy a shared fantasy mind-state. They might share many mundane concerns, such as childcare, finances and unfinished to-do lists, which can creep into the ambiance. The more unresolved issues there are in the relationship, whether mundane or profound, the harder it may be to leave that behind to enjoy play. The longer the relationship lasts and the more intertwined the people in it become, the more shared concerns accumulate that must be set aside for them to play freely. In new or casual relationships, the obstacles of day-to-day life are small or non-existent, allowing for an easier shift to play headspace. This is not a trust issue but an issue of failure to transition headspace effectively. If, however, this is combined with greater ease and frequency of play with people outside of the primary relationship, then jealousy, envy and suspicion can rear their ugly green heads. Now, what was previously an issue of transition becomes an issue of trust.

Along with the creeping reality of to-do lists entering the fantasy realm, over-familiarity in itself may reduce the thrill of SM for some people. This can take two different courses; getting stuck in a rut and trusting too much.

After a long time together, even the most intense play partners can experience some sense of routine, perhaps even feeling like they're in a bad rut. While we seek comfort in consistency and reliability, there comes a time when that may turn into boredom. For occasional players, scenes that follow a similar flow might eventually leave one or both of the parties unfulfilled. Even for 'lifestyle' players, what seemed at first like a revolutionary act of entering into a D/s relationship, with it's rigidly defined roles, may at some time down the road, seem suffocatingly predictable. The simple answer seems to be to change the type of play. Consider, however, the perceived risks discussed earlier – the risk of losing the relationship as it stands. A change to the status quo can be very threatening if there's the possibility of a considerable downside. Some may feel that a rut may be better than failure, thus they are willing to endure slowly mounting frustrations. The problem is that this frustration eventually leaks out. Even the most empathetic partner may interpret the signs of frustration as rejection or lack of attraction. It's easy to take something like this personally. The frustrated person may find it easier to blame the other as well.

Some people are surprise junkies. They love the unknown, even in their sexuality. Most people seek ways to reduce senseless or excessive risk in sexual adventures yet still find ways to feed their desire for the exotic, unknown and surprising. Some people are willing to go home with a stranger they met at a bar and try kinky sex with them. Others are willing to play with new acquaintances as a semi public party but would never imagine the bar pick-up scenario. But for both of these types of people, the element of surprise is essential. There's a subcategory of the surprise junkies – the fear feeders. They crave an edge of fear to feel vibrantly alive. For fear feeders, too much trust dulls the erotic potential of an interaction. The more entwined their lives become with their partner's, the deeper and stronger the trust becomes. Most fear feeders do genuinely appreciate their partnerships. Often it's only in a limited part of their lives, such as their sex life, that they feel a sense of dissatisfaction if they believe that their play is entirely risk free. Even if it's simply a perceived fear thanks to an active imagination and a well fleshed-out role playing scene, they need to have some sense of real risk involved, an arena where there's just a touch of doubt on trust. On this perceived sliver of danger they can find thrill. They suffocate in predictability and in the assurance of 100% safety. Give them a 0.01% possibility of danger and they perk right up! How do you know if someone's an erotic fear feeder? Perhaps an examination of other activities that give them pleasure might give a clue. Consider if you will the backcountry skiers, skydivers, horror movie lovers and day traders… or endorphin junkies in general.

Jo and Jane's situation is not simple. But it's probably not as dismal as they may feel at times. If they are capable of discussing frankly what perceived risks cause them to hesitate in play, then they have a strong chance at finding a new course of SM play explorations. When the discussion of trust is broken down first to the level of perceived risk analysis, it's much easier to not take it personally and to make positive changes in the situation.

In following essays we'll look further into the issue to trust, vulnerability and SM/Ds by discussing Mark - the popular single guy, the master without a slave and the single female submissive.

Trust, Vulnerability and SM/Ds Part 2

Trust is an integral part of SM. There's no denying this statement. After all, in today's loosely knit, enormous network of people we call the SM community, we fiercely adhere to the credo of "Safe, Sane and Consensual." It's taught in all the classes and it's in all the books. Underlying this very sensible motto is the assumption of trust. We trust that the person we play with has safe techniques. We trust that they are in their right mind. We trust that they will respect our limits and seek our consent. Yet we don't often discuss what it really means to trust in SM and D/s. By what criteria will we trust and for what range of activities?

Not all SM encounters happen with long-time committed partners. It's not unusual for people to play with friends, occasional lovers, casual acquaintances or even near strangers. Many SM activities can be potentially dangerous to the body, and many D/s experiences can be emotionally perilous if poorly executed. Given this, it may seem foolish that people would play with near strangers and casual acquaintances. Yet there are socially sanctioned arenas in which this happens every day without too much concern. The semi-public SM play party is one, the professional SM session is another.

Let's recall one of our case studies mentioned in the last essay: Mike, the handsome guy who calls on a favorite professional dominant. Consider if you will, dear readers, what is not said here. What Mike has not mentioned is that he probably knows even less about the dom than the dom knows of him. How is it possible that Mike can trust this stranger with his physical safety and the emotional vulnerability of submission? One would think that the initial criterion of the sexy photo is a wholly inadequate means of judging a trustworthy top. This makes sense. After all there is no correlation between good looks and great SM skills. Let's not forget, however, that Mike also made a decision to hire a professional SM practitioner, not just a pretty face at the bar. .

To examine trust and SM in a professional context we still need to look at what the perceived risk is. Like any other SM encounter, physical and emotional safety is a risk. There's also the risk that the professional does not have "what it takes" for the experience to be exciting. This point is much harder to pinpoint as it's quite subjective.

By choosing to seek out a professional SM practitioner, Mike's made certain assumptions and decisions around trust, risk and his own priorities. By the very commercial nature of professional dominance, a branch of the sex industry, the consumer assumes that there's at least a basic level of technical competence for the pro to stay in business. (While this is a sensible assumption, unfortunately for many consumers, it's often not true.) The level of excellence, of course, will vary and is likely reflected in the level of demand that the professional enjoys. Mike has assumed that the professional's longevity in the business speaks well of skill and desirability. Mike also decided that appearance was an important factor in his turn-on and submission headspace, and he trusts that the photo in the ad is a current and accurate representation.

Beyond the technical competence and truth in advertising, Mike also assumes that he can trust the professional to respect his boundaries of confidentiality and emotional limits. He trusts that the relationship will remain within the context of the professional interaction and that the intense connection and experience shared in the session will not spill over to the wider scope of their personal lives.

At this point we need to consider why he's going to a professional and not seeking SM play in his private life. The reasons for seeking professional SM services vary from person to person. He might be in a social circle where no one, to the best of his knowledge, plays in the way he wants to. In other words, he has lovers that he could trust with his life and emotional vulnerability but not with the skill needed to wield a whip upon his flesh. He may also find it really tiresome to go through the whole cruising, courtship and mating dance to find a compatible lover... and then to put his selection through the even narrower filter

83

of the kink factor. He can, however, trust the professional to know their way around the dungeon. The consumer may be in a situation in which, for whatever reason, he needs to keep his kinky desires private and not share them with lovers for friends. He can trust a good professional with discretion, privacy and confidentiality. He may fear that his lovers and partners might judge him harshly or reject him for his needs and wants. He believes that the professionals will not. They've seen everything, he figures. It can be difficult and embarrassing to bring up pervy desires with lovers, but the professional should be able to provide a relaxed and non-judgmental atmosphere to talk about even the oddest of lusts.

In our last installment we looked at the needs of those we call "surprise junkies" and "fear feeders." These are the players who find thrill, arousal and a vivid sense of being alive when faced with a real or perceived uncertainty and a touch of danger. The semi-stranger status and the mystique of the leather clad and whip wielding dominant, in itself, may be the thrill of the experience that simply cannot be met by a totally familiar face. So they may call upon a professional, to balance the need for the thrill of uncertainly without risking play with a potential psycho picked up at a leather bar.

For some SM consumers, their need for kink, SM and D/s may be a very significant element of their sexuality, yet one that really needs to be fed only on an occasional basis. If so, why should they put the added pressure of technical competence and emotional acceptance on their partners? Some people just want the occasional play session without wanting to dive into the churning sea of the leather community. They want the fun but not the commitment to a leather life or the accountability to a group of people bound together only by a mutual affinity for a sexual style. If that's the case, they can trust that a professional will not want to develop a significant primary relationship with them or wish to know all about him and enter their private life. They only need to reveal what is relevant to them for the scope of the interaction around a session. This is not to say that the professional and client cannot have a sincere and personable relationship. They can and many do. Many people also develop friendships with their doctors and accountants, yet are able to understand the boundaries of professional and personal interactions.

There is also a unique honesty and trust created by the anonymity and professional context of the client-pro relationship. Because the other arenas of life are not intertwined between the two, unlike with two partnered players, certain risks are removed. The question of "can I face this person in the morning and enjoy our egalitarian relationship after I reveal my dark desire?" does not enter into the equation here. Judgment is not an issue. They are also not expected to adhere to codes of behavior befitting their social station or occupational position. Because of this, many consumers of professional SM services feel a sense of emotional safety and they feel they can trust that the pro will not reject or ridicule them. In a sense, there is a safety of the confessional created within the four dungeon walls. It is not relevant whether the names they use in the outside world are used or not, it's not relevant that a person behave according to their station in life, and it's certainly not relevant that they adhere to social codes of dignity and shame should they not want to. A mutual suspension of disbelief in the existence of an outside life creates this odd situation where certain honesties can flourish. The client can trust the professional to accept the nakedness of his soul... if that's what he needs. In the client-professional relationship, an unusual situation is created. Mike might not be able to trust his dom with his name and identity, but he can trust the pro to care for his flesh and soul.

Trust is an odd thing, isn't it?

Trust, Vulnerability and SM/Ds Part 3

We continue with this third part in a series of discussions on the nature of trust. Today let's consider our remaining cases, as we look further into the issue of trust and vulnerability in SM/Ds. Remember Master X, who wants to find a full-time submissive?

Recently there's been a surge of interest in what various sectors of the SM community call 24/7 D/s, Total Power Exchange, Master/slave relationships and so on – various expressions of full time committed dominant / submissive relationships. Perhaps it's part of the process of change and cycles within the community, however, I find it interesting that it was just a few years ago that those who sought Master / slave relationships were considered a bit batty even in the Safe/Sane/ Consensual world. They were treated a bit like the crazy aunt in the attic of polite SM society. Then, somewhere along the way the romance of the 'lifestyle' bloomed, again. For whatever the cause, the shift of interest toward extended D/s has been rapid and has moved forward in many cases without the guiding hand of generational experience. It's not that this form of relationship is a new thing. It's just that the earlier generations of practitioners are often not among us: age, retirement, burnout and AIDS have taken their toll among the ranks of our would-be teachers.

So, what does this have to do with our Master X., trust and SM? The poor guy is doing the best he can to create the relationship he fantasizes about. The only tools he can come up with are to directly transfer the methods of short scenes to an extended relationship. He doesn't have the experiences, both delightful and devastating, of our predecessors to draw from. The tool he has doesn't transfer to this new sort of relationship or help to foster a different range of trust required in it. He doesn't even realize this. How can he, in a world filled with fantasy, fiction and misinformation?

As we discussed earlier in the case of Mike, individual scenes can be compartmentalized from the rest of the players' lives and thus the scope of trust required becomes specific and limited to the activities and the limited relationship within that specific play scene. More simply put, when people converge just for play, whether they go to a professional or play privately, they're primarily concerned about whether they can trust the other with the skills and emotional caring required for a fulfilling scene. They are not, however, worried about whether they can trust the other with making decisions that affect their career, family and life goals. So, they are able to trust a person deeply within the limited and very specific context of a scene – and that in itself may be the catharsis that the modern citizen, weary of the world around them, seeks. In the scope of such play, the extent of the Self invested in that experience is also defined and limited. This also offers the players freedom to express themselves as concentrated and focused 'personas' in that scene; one is free to be a Master, a Mistress, a sissy, a boy, a dog, etc. But in the long-term committed relationship, more of the partner's Self become intertwined in ways that are broader and deeper. With this added dimension of greater involvement of the Self in a leather relationship, also comes greater risks of wound to the core self. No longer can the Self be protected through compartmentalization. Now, every interaction puts the totality of both individuals on the line. When this realization of this risk becomes clearer through the fog of romantic notions, there are three courses for the participants to take. Turn and run, lash out to protect themselves or surrender deeply and trust in a way that they've never trusted before.

The last option is hard enough to achieve even under vanilla circumstances. It usually takes time for both to come to grips with the responsibility accorded to both the dominant and the submissive. Yet, in so many new relationships, such as the ones Master X. has attempted, the two people rush in to mimic storybook fantasies with the speed and rigidity of single evening scenes. It's such a seductive scenario to leave convention behind and dive into the world of no-holds-barred 24/7 Ds. I congratulate them for being willing to pursue their dreams. The question is, are they aware of the risks inherent in this chosen path as well as the potential joy? It is not beyond most willing participants' ability to be 100% alert to their dominant's needs for a couple of hours, a weekend or even a week; likewise, it's reasonably possible to be the decisive, perfect and strong Master for the same amount of time. It would, however, take the discipline and dedication of the fervently devout to do so for a year, much less a lifetime. On top of that, the Ds relationship must function fully outside of the cocoon of the play party and leather world, in a larger society that not only will not understand the participants, but will be hostile to their chosen roles and identities.

The reality is that here are two people who will have to journey together to redefine the protocols, dynamics and workings of their relationship to optimize each person's full potential in a hostile world, where working role models are scarce at best. They are on their own. They also have to trust one another to make decisions beyond safe SM practices, such as money, career, childrearing and all the mundane stuff of life that have to be defined and duties that must be separated within the doctrine of D/s. Yes, I think it might be hard to find the right person that you can trust to achieve something so unusual together.

So then, is the full-time, long-term D/s the mythical unicorn of the SM world? No, I don't think so. But it's as rare as a white tiger and needs just as much respect and trust when handling it.

Shifting gears a bit, let's consider 'Beth.' The professional woman and well trained, seasoned submissive who met the dominant on-line, and planned on traveling alone across the country for a few days of full submission and play scene with her virtual Dom. Her friends scold her that this goes against all teachings about proper Safe / Sane and Consensual SM practice. What about the check-in? What about the detailed negotiation? What about meeting in a public place? Surely, they all chide her, nothing good could come of her suddenly taking leave of her senses and good judgment. She must be protected, this must be stopped.

Has she lost her mind? Probably not.

While it's lovely and caring of her friends to be so concerned for her welfare, they seem to be forgetting something…. Beth is an adult capable of making adult decisions of levels of risk she can accept to live her life fully. There's been a disturbing trend within some parts of the SM community to micro-legislate safe behavior, and thereby necessarily dictating how trust must be established between two consenting adults.

Over the course of time, such attempts to mandate proper sex behavior within the alternative community can reduce perfectly mature and capable adults to a place of childish helplessness when it comes to sexual autonomy. The ugly underlying message of such communal ordinances is that the individual cannot be trusted to make decisions for his or her own best interest. Beth's desire to enjoy submission and her self-identification as a submissive does not equal immaturity, dependency or the inability to make decisions. It troubles me when I see people behave as though this were the case, especially when thinking about themselves. When an individual's decision making, risk assessment and trust assessment stops being measured not by their internal yardstick, and becomes dependant on the external formulas of the community, the community is doing the individual a grave disservice.

In Beth's case, I hope that her friends have been listening to her talk about how her long distance relationship had been coming along, so that they might be aware of any emotional or behavioral red flags. If they are truly concerned, then they should voice them to her as concerns, but not try to dictate her adult decisions. Then, after that, I would hope that they would make themselves available for any help or support she might want, instead of casting judgment upon her.

For now, I reluctantly bring this discussion of trust, vulnerability and risk assessment in SM and D/s to a close. There is much more to say, and individual experience varies widely... I have simply attempted to provide some food for thought.

Aftercare: Healing Better to Play Harder

In my travels in the SM/Leather community, I've noticed an increasing interest in more intense play. This isn't surprising as the transmission of knowledge is more geometric rather than linear. A greater number of people are becoming more technically skilled and better informed about SM. Leather community conferences, classes, books and the internet have all added to this. This is neither good nor bad. It simply is.

As we play harder than ever before, are we recovering, healing and growing better than before? As we seek greater adventures in kinky play, do we remember that the potential jarring to the body, mind and heart may be deeper than before? Are we paying attention to what happens after a scene, not just how to create one that's technically proficient? Are we minding our aftercare as well as we should?

I realize that aftercare isn't as sexy of a topic as say, double handed flogging, Master/slave protocols, suspension bondage, etc. Thus we don't see it talked about often in educational series or discussed in depth. We know we need it, but we don't dwell on it. We treat it like flossing our teeth. "Yes, yes, we know..." Unfortunately the reality is that the presence or absence of aftercare, and its timing, quality and sincerity of aftercare can make the difference between a fantastic scene and a miserable experience. It's as necessary as air or water; similarly vital, yet taken for granted until it goes missing or quality is degraded.

There are several different varieties and phases of aftercare.

At the most basic is the human courtesy to acknowledge the end of the scene and the other's contribution to both of your experiences. Suddenly halting a scene without cool down or mutual sense of closure can feel as jarring as getting read-ended while cruising along the freeway at 70mph. Whatever wonderful experience you may have been having is now wrecked. Regardless of the pleasure they took during the experience, the other person is uncertain as to the reason for its end and may take the blame or resent the other. You wouldn't screw a person, cum and just withdraw your organ and leave without saying anything, would you? At least you'd say "Bye." Just because a person is a submissive, a masochist, a sadist or a dominant doesn't mean they don't respond as any other person would to moments of intense intimacy. SM for some is more intimate then sex.

Aftercare Phase 1: Physical Recovery

A basic level of aftercare is the physical recovery. This is when we put Humpty Dumpty together again. If there are cuts, clean them and cover them. If the body is cold, hungry or hurt, fix it. Most people find it appropriate to stay with the person long enough to make certain that they are able to operate heavy machinery, i.e. their car. For some, this recovery time is a matter of minutes, for others it might take a few hours. This is all common sense stuff. Other than specific first aid, possible medical information and willingness to hang out while the 'high' wears off, not much is needed to figure out thus far.

Let's call all this Phase 1 of Aftercare. It's the immediate and basic physical recovery and emotional cool-down time. If you've been playing for a while you'll probably have a general idea of how you like your aftercare. It's really a matter of personal preference. Some like lots of physical contact while others do not. Some are very chatty and others prefer quiet. Some want to spend time with their play partner, join others or be left alone. Some take a long time, while others bounce from one scene to another scene or engage in a new activity with barely a breath. Since aftercare needs vary so much, I highly suggest that you take inventory of how you like your aftercare and mention it to your play partner. The general duration of your aftercare should be built into the overall timing consideration for a scene. If you generally need 2 hours for aftercare and you only have 3 hours together, then that leaves an hour for play. Failing to plan this might leave one or all players out in the cold without good aftercare. If you have 3 hours together and you play for 2 hours and 45 minutes, and then two hours of aftercare isn't going to fit into 15 minutes. That makes for a very difficult transition from the land of pleasure and fantasy to the harsh reality of driving home.

Here's a jewel of a little kinky sex secret: Fantastic aftercare, (what that is varies from person to person of course) can make a mediocre scene seem glowingly wonderful. A terrible aftercare experience or absence of aftercare entirely can turn an amazing scene experience into a horrible one. Now you see why it's worth investigating what your partner's aftercare needs are. It might be the difference between you being a stud or a dud.

For some folks, good sex is good aftercare, or even the goal of the whole experience! And that's just wonderful! For others, they have no interest in aftercare of the other person and that's just how they are. Does that make them a bad SM person? That depends on how they deal with their preference. It's perfectly fine to state, during negotiation for play, that they don't provide aftercare. Then it's out in the open and the other person can choose how to proceed. Maybe they choose not to play or choose to play anyway. Maybe the other person will forgo aftercare or arrange to get it from someone else. If, however, the person who won't provide aftercare fails to mention that in advance and the scene ends in totally conflicted aftercare expectations, we have a problem.

Aftercare Phase 2: Check-in

Let me introduce to you Phase 2. We in the leather community often talk about a "check-in call" the next day. Why is this needed and what is accomplished by this? What really needs to take place in this conversation? How should the check-in call be conducted? Well, since I'm not one to legislate behavior, I'll simply bring up some thoughts and ideas on this.

It's quite common with kinky play, whether it's physically or emotionally intense, to feel a huge adrenaline rush and shift of neural chemicals of various sorts during play. (Well, actually, I hope this happens most of the time for you. After all, the adrenaline goes hand in hand with pleasure.) As the scene closes and we "return to earth," the level of adrenaline, endorphins, serotonin and other yummy body chemicals come down. Sometimes it's a nice slow easing off from a state of ecstatic pleasure, leaving us in a place of soft contentment. Sometimes the shift is fast and sudden enough to leave a person's body and mind in a state much like a miniature version of shock. In theory, if this mini shock can happen during the basic, post-scene physical care and maintenance level of aftercare, then it's all groovy. We can take care of it right along with the bruises. Unfortunately, human behavior rarely follows theory. When and how we come down from the "high" of flying in a wonderful scene is not entirely predictable. More experienced players have enough personal data to know their general patterns, but there's always room for surprises. Sometimes we are moved deeper and fly higher than either party expected. So, it's not uncommon that we experience a "drop" the next day, or for that matter, several days after the scene. This may leave us in various states of emotional dishevelment. Various feelings may arise after personally or physically significant scene experiences: Anxiety, moodiness, agitation, anger, lethargy, loneliness, fatigue, disorientation, indecisiveness, etc. etc. Needless to say, this is not a fun place to be in. Check-ins are a way of grounding us back to calm and solidity when the storm of feelings uproot us.

A check-in call gives a chance for the players to connect after bit of time has passed during which post-scene emotions have emerged and been processed, or at least have begun to be processed, after a scene. It may be that both parties are perfectly fine and they had a nice "soft landing" without feelings getting stirred up. If that's the case, then great! Then the check-in call can serve as way to thank one another for the shared pleasure, trade compliments and express your pleasure with the experience. If it's considered polite to call to thank the host after a dinner invitations, it's certainly polite to do so after such an intimate invitation as one for SM play. If all is good, you may also use this call to set up a potential follow-up date. If one or both people are feeling a drop from a scene, however, the check-in call becomes more important. Sometimes, a simple expression of reassurance, gratitude and validation from the other person may relieve the post-scene blues. We all seek validation, affection and a sense of worth. The body chemical drop may amplify the profound vulnerability created in play, carrying it over to the next day. The emotional nakedness that the person experienced may leave them anxious about potentially being judged negatively, or worse, of being rejected. These concerns are often soothed by the conscientious play-partner in the check-in call. The conversation also gives the caller more insight into the psychological structure of the other person—critical pieces of information for creating hotter scenes or safer experiences with them in the future.

What if we have the check-in call and need to say things that aren't all great? What if something bad happened in the scene and you're not happy or feel somehow endangered or mistreated? What if you felt that it wasn't what you wanted after all? What if physical problems came up that needed medical attention? What if you have to listen to a negative post scene conversation? It happens. We need to get tools to deal with this.

First of all, we're all adults. Whether or not the scene went well, both people entered into it as equal human beings with consent. If one felt that they had no power to consent to entering into the scene, then this is no longer SM. It just might be called abuse. Since both have consented, both have accepted responsibilities. If a scene didn't work out, before you complain or blame, you have to take inventory. Where did it go wrong? Who shares the responsibility, and how? Were communications clear enough? Did the two of you mean the same thing by the terms used?

Some questions you might want to ask yourself before going into discussing the scene that didn't work...

- What am I feeling?
- When did that feeling start?
- Did I assess my needs, wants and limits clearly before playing?
- Did I communicate these needs, wants and limits clearly before playing?
- Did I understand the other person's needs, wants and desires clearly?
- When things went wrong, did I communicate that to the other person once I realized it?
- Was the bad thing that happened part of what I considered acceptable risk in this scene?
- Was my appetite greater than my ability to fulfill it?
- What was my intent in the scene?
- What was the other person's intent in the scene?
- How big of a deal is this negative experience relative to the whole scene and / or relationship to the person?
- What further care do I need to feel whole or complete again?
- Did I communicate my aftercare needs to my partner before the scene began?

Remember to talk about how *you* are feeling. "I'm feeling down after our scene" is very different then "You made me feel crappy from that scene." Don't make blaming statements. Speak with compassion, and remember that it's very difficult for the other to feel judged or criticized. They may be just as raw and vulnerable as you are. Whatever you do, don't hold in the negative feelings and resent them in silence. It's not fair to the other person or yourself if you deny the chance to clear the air and gain better understanding. It's also very childish.

Have you noticed that I've been generally avoiding the use of the terms top, bottom, dominant or submissive so far? One might think that aftercare is only for bottoms and submissives, but it's also for tops, sadists and dominants. Tops go through similarly intense changes in their body chemistry, leading to the potential shock-like emotional and physical crashes. Beyond the fundamental physiological concerns, most often the top has their sense of Self and self-worth wrapped up in the scene as much as the bottom does. In the act of sadism or dominance the top has exposed their desires and hungers, which aren't necessarily socially acceptable. We've been taught not to hit those we love. Now we do it for fun. It can take a bit of mental contortion to reconcile the cognitive dissonance with this. Many tops want to know that they are still loved and desired after exposing their darker desires. Their pride as a technician and lover may also be involved in this. The top wants validation that they were a "good top." Telling a top that "Your flogging sucks" just might crush them. Even if they look pissed off, they're actually hurt. You might not get another date or you may have stunted their growth as a top with such a statement. Instead you might want to say: "Thanks for flogging me! I think maybe that flogger's a bit too much for our scenes. Let's go shopping for a new flogger just for us." (Then you go and get a good practice flogger you like that they can't damage you with if they tried.)

Here's an interesting insight into Top psychology: there are times when the bottom needs very little aftercare, but the top insists upon it. For many tops, providing aftercare for the bottom may be exactly the aftercare that they need. The act of providing help and healing allows many tops to feel whole, compassionate, kind and validated. This may be how they balance for the darker side that they expressed earlier in scene. So what do you do if you're the bottom and you feel like you're done with your aftercare but the top is still fussing over you? If you can, let them, and understand that you're doing their aftercare in letting them provide for you.

Not all aftercare needs to happen with the person you played with. It may not be possible or it may not be desirable. If you hooked up with someone at a bar and played in the back alley or at a sex/SM club, you may not have their contact info. You may not even want to know their name. You may have hired a professional dominant but you don't want aftercare with them. You may be a professional dominant and can't contact your client for aftercare for them or yourself, or you may find that's beyond the professional relationship the two of you set up. For so many reasons, aftercare doesn't have to be with the person you played with.

Aftercare Phase 3: Deeper Aftercare

Maybe you didn't realize you needed deeper aftercare until well after your partner was unreachable or reasonably available. Or maybe you need therapeutic attention. If you need special aftercare, you need it, and there's no question about that. Now we're getting into Phase 3 – the tar pit of emotions that can bubble up once in a while with SM play. Phase 3 doesn't always happen but it can and if not dealt with, it'll swallow you up or get in the way of your relationship with the other person. This is one of the many reasons why it's important to have folks in your life with whom you can talk about your kinky life. You have to figure out how much aftercare you can reasonably ask of that third party caregiver. Sometimes the care you need may be deep enough for you to consider a therapist or other professional listener/healer/consoler. Some issues that can come up with play may be simply beyond the capability of your play partner or third party.

Maybe you engaged in intense play as a performance or commercial exchange. You might do live SM shows on stage or via the Web, you might be shooting a SM porno video, you might be doing a show on a fetish event stage. Is there a responsibility for aftercare in such a situation? If so, where does it lie? A producer has certain expectations of professionalism on the performer's part. Yet they are dealing with human beings in very intense situations. Even the military has built-in means for post-combat emotional care. At a strictly Machiavellian level, isn't it in the best interest of the commercial producer to clean up the state of mind of the performer as they would clean up the video footage and equipment afterwards? Or is it?

Something for all of us to ponder…

Quick Guide: After Care Suggestions
Here are some things to consider or include as you see fit:

- *Phase 0*
    o   When: Before playing
    o   Assess what you like for general aftercare and share
        with playmate.
        ◉   Touch and physical contact?
        ◉   Talkative or not?
        ◉   Food needs?
        ◉   Special medical or physical considerations?
        ◉   How much time do you usually want? Make
            sure to plan in time for aftercare before getting
            started!
        ◉   Both tops and bottoms have aftercare needs.
    o   Find out what your partner wants or needs in terms of
        aftercare.
    o   Can you provide for each other's aftercare?
    o   If not, who is available to provide it?

- *Phase 1*
    o   When: Immediately after play
    o   Mutual understanding that the scene is over.
    o   Patching up the scrapes and bruises.
    o   Let the body and mind recover from the adventures.
    o   Sharing the afterglow. Let the partner know that you
        had a good time.
    o   Critiques? Might want to keep it until later.
    o   Arrange for check-in if needed. (When, How, Where)

- *Phase 2*
    o   When: Generally within days of the scene.
    o   Check in as per your agreement. Don't blow this off if
        you set it up.
    o   The Good Stuff: Acknowledge, thank and enjoy the
        memories of a good time.
    o   Critiques: Be gentle and considerate. Don't hide and
        resent.
    o   Possibly begin discussions for next time.

- *Phase 3*
  - o When: Days, months, years,
  - o Identify the problem.
  - o Whose issue is the problem? (Yours, play partner, facility owner, etc.)
  - o Who is best equipped to help you deal with this? (The play partner, lover, friend, mentor, therapist, medical professional, etc.)
  - o Deal with the problem or challenge. Don't stuff it.

Chastity: The Process of Discovering Pleasure in Power

Many, many moons ago, when I was just a baby femme top trying to make my first few tentative steps towards dominance, I took possession of a lover of mine for two weeks as my slave. Although I was new to running scenes, I wasn't new to SM. Having spent a great deal of my bottom time as an unrepentant pig and demanding do-me-queen, I felt that I also had a pretty clear sense of what I wanted to do as a top in the arena of bondage and sensation play.

Then he threw me a curve ball. He wanted to engage in "chastity play."

My response: "Huh?"

He wanted me to take control of his sexual pleasure and deny him orgasm.

"Ok", I thought. "I don't quite understand the motivation, but it seems clear enough in method to get started." I figured that I was supposed to deny him orgasm and sensual genital touch for the entire two weeks of his service to me. It wasn't any skin off my back, since I could still flog him, spank him, play with all forms of sensations, creative bondage, mummification and even golden shower play. So, I simply ignored his penis for the contracted service time. Like I said, it wasn't any trouble for me. After all, I had no issues with taking responsibility for my own pleasures and his cock wasn't the source of my pleasure. I love my clit and I know what a vibrator is for.

Towards the middle of two weeks he began to complain about not getting sensual attention. I ignored his appeals, as I was convinced that this was part of the chastity game to play along with. I figured that when he whined and complained about it, I was to deny his desperate plea for blue-ball release. Steeling myself to his ever-amplifying petitions, I continued to not allow him any release or pay attention to his genitals, whatsoever.

Towards the end of the two weeks he continued to complain, becoming grumpy and very disgruntled by the whole chastity ordeal. At the end we had a conversation that went something like this.

Him: "You wouldn't touch me." (sad look)
Me: "You wanted chastity play."(matter-of-fact look)
Him: "Yes, but I didn't get to come." (pained look)
Me: "That's what you wanted, right?" (confused look)
Him: "But when was I going to get to come?" (deeper pained look)
Me: "Why would you get to come in chastity play?" (deeper confused look)
Him: Because there's no fun if I didn't get to!" (near desperate look)
Me: "Then why did you want me to deny you orgasms?" (utterly boggled look)
Him: "Because I thought it would be hot." (incredulous look)
Me: "So, it wasn't"? (perplexed dog with peanut buttered mouth look)
Him: "No! Not after two weeks!" (definitely desperate look)
Me: "I gave you exactly what you asked for. If it turns out that you don't want what it is that you're asking me for, then I have no idea how to play with you. You don't want attention on your penis, and then you tell me that's all you were looking for.... Forget it."

If we weren't each so hurt and confused, we would have been rolling on the floor laughing from the dialogue the same way you are...

Needless to say, this scene was not repeated again for a very long time. In hindsight I realized that, at the time, neither of us had the capability to deconstruct the superficial aspect of the chastity scene to extract the core desire. We were also in a time and place (pre-internet and before a plethora of SM seminars became available) where few around us could discuss and shed light upon the subtler aspects of chastity play.

Occasionally after that I would run into people, mainly men but some women, who wanted to engage in what they called "chastity play." Upon discussion of their motivations, I would invariably discover that they simply wanted an elaborately ritualized tease-and-denial that to me seemed to require a paradoxically intense focus on their genitals. Their vision of chastity play didn't appeal my desire for deep control. But they insisted that what they described was chastity play. This always left me feeling let down and feeling a bit put-upon, as if I were simply a blank slate of desire on which they could project their fantasies. I wasn't sure if it was worse when I felt that they were ignoring my vision of chastity play or when they assumed how I might take pleasure from the experience.

Being the good egghead, however, I tried to wrap my mind around it, but alas, to my great disappointment, I could never reconcile their fantasy from what looked to me like selfishness.

In short, I was annoyed.

Then I met Gumby. He gave me the sort of education for a top that only the most insightful bottom can give: deep knowledge and honest perspective from the heart of the submissive. He was the first submissive in my exploration of chastity play who placed the dominant's needs and desires at the center of the chastity play focus and not the anatomy in question. He was on loan to me from his lovely mistress/ wife. I will always thank her for her generosity.

He told me about the great emotional vulnerability that a dom can create in a sub through chastity play that leads to deepening the power exchange in the relationship. At first I was skeptical. Then he showed me just how true it could be during his times of submission to me. Something clicked for me.

Fast-forward a bit....

I had occasion to play with the earlier mentioned lover with whom I had the unsuccessful original chastity scene with. He had taken the initiative and bought a CB2000 - a clear Lucite contraption that resembles a miniature South-East Asian fish trap with a padlock. I expressed interest in bringing that into our play. Remembering the

101

original disaster, he quickly declined. He heard an audible sigh of disappointment from me. A few days later he called me back with a change of heart. "If this would make you really happy, I'm willing to try it." Suddenly I found myself keenly interested in play with him in an entirely fresh way. I was so perked up by this that even I was surprised by my newfound attitude.

The weekend play date came around. He presented himself to me with the device already clamped on for nearly a week. He'd had this on for me, he told me. My heart leapt a bit, as if we were new lovers again - an odd feeling, but nice and refreshing at the same time. I asked him if he was really ready to commit to the boundaries that he'd agreed to. With the exception of an injury related limitation, he was utterly mine to do what I wished with. Something in his tone told me that he's serious in a way that he's never been. I asked him again, if he was sure. He confirmed without hesitation. The key is transferred to my possession.

Over the course of that weekend, I took great delight in doing exactly what I pleased. Our negotiation was complete and final with one limit and one consent at the very beginning. I took this to heart.

What I discovered that weekend was a great joy of very real control over a fully consenting submissive. The chastity device, when applied with clarity of intent, became the fulcrum around which my power was magnified. He was very turned on by my dominance, which would in turn made him hard, and then extremely uncomfortable. That cycle would emphasize his state of submission even more in his head. His arousal did not come from any genital contact, but from simply watching me take my own pleasure from him in so many ways. I delighted in his vulnerability and in the docile demeanor the device created in him. I would lead him through activities that, in our previous scenes and circumstances, would take a great deal of careful negotiation before, and management during play, to achieve. Yet, when an absolute consent was granted in the beginning of the scene, we were permitted to both unflinchingly leap off the cliff of pleasure and desire without small-stepped hesitations.

You might imagine that I committed all forms of sexual and sadistic atrocities upon him. Actually, the activities were not all that edgy. We did the usual light bondage, sweet flogging, kneeling at feet, relaxing as he prepared my bath, etc. (OK, so the ornamental cutting scene with my mark and several multi layered piercings was a bit intense...) I also made him watch a movie of my selection, not our selection. I made him skate in the park with me. I specified when he'd wake, when he should awaken me, how to prepare breakfast, and how to serve it to me. These were simple but significant pleasures for me. Each of my commands and directions were given, and taken, with the knowledge of my absolute authority in the relationship. I have known for a long time how much I enjoyed that form of intense and intimate relationship. Unfortunately it's not too common to find another who will sincerely enjoy the reciprocal space, unhesitatingly and over a long period of time. Not only did he obey me, but he obeyed willingly, and with each act of obedience, he found himself turned on by attention that was not necessarily directly sexual but erotic in its own way.

Today I have a full time D/s relationship with a boy servant who always attends to such things for me. You'd think that the scene with a lover would not be a big deal for me now, but what he gave me years ago was unique. I am not, however, discounting or minimizing the wonderful service and submission that my servant provides me today. Quite the contrary, I treasure it. What was so interesting about the pleasure taken from the early scene with the lover described above, was that he had been a lover and a masochist play buddy, not a submissive first. The chastity play drew out a new depth of submission previously unknown to him and certainly to the relationship, even if for a very limited time.

Over the past few years, I have come to realize that one of my great pleasures in dominance is to have a person do for me what he or she would not do for others. The lover has never given this form of submission to anyone else, and the boy servant is devoted and attentive to me in a way that she is to no other.

Chastity play has become an effective physical and psychological tool by which I can achieve an intimate D/s power dynamic. The chastity device itself has taken on a ritualized and symbolic value for me that it did not previously have.

Ever since the lesson I learned from Gumby and the gestalt weekend of deep D/s with my lover, I've delighted and toyed with elements of chastity as an expression of power: making my servant sleep with bondage mittens, mailing chastity instructions to my lovers, considering permanent chastity locks on a slave's labia, and more.

It's amazing how a shift in perspective can refresh one's play. In the end, it's not what you do, but why you do it that makes all the difference in SM and D/s.

Pussy Play For Control "Take Cuntrol"

So you got her as your pleasure slave for the evening. She's wearing your collar. Naked and willing, she's kneeling before you. What are you gonna' do? Pull out your big cock and tell her, "suck my dick, slave girl!" ? Oh that's really creative.... Hardly. You'll blow your dominant wad in five minutes and be done for the evening. You've just wasted a whole evening of her submission to you. Do you want to get all you can out of the evening? Invest your time wisely. Motivate her to want to serve you well.

Take cuntrol! It's time to lean about cunt play and pussy torment.

You know that your dick controls you. It's a bit more complicated with women, but if you get the knack for it, you too can lead her by her libido.

Here's the big secret with cunt play. In order to motivate properly, first you must be able to create mind-blowing pleasure before denial, teasing or torment can be effective. If she knows that you hold to power to send her into Nirvana, then and only then will cunt torment hold the potential for pleasure for her. Otherwise she might as well just call the safe-word and watch TV. It's easy to think that pussy torment is just about causing pain in the naughty bits. It's more than that. Cunt torment without the ability to pleasure her is artless brutality. You gotta' know how to make a pussy purr before you can make it growl.

Now that we've established that basic rule, let me share some steamy ideas so you can take proper cuntrol of your submissive. Once the scene is underway, order her to present her cunt to you. This might make her a bit embarrassed. That's good. Now you have the psychological upper hand because she's a bit flustered and off balance. Sexual embarrassment like this can be hot for a lot of women. Is she showing herself a bit too demurely for your taste? Did she not lift her skirt high enough? Were her legs not spread far enough? Make her do it over again until you're satisfied with her performance.

Whether or not you put her in bondage at this time is up to you. You know that I love bondage. I would take this opportunity to tie her legs apart for better access and increased sense of vulnerability.

Once you feel satisfied with how she's presented herself to you, then inspect what she's offering. Take a close look. Move the skin of the labia around. Make her spread her lips for you. Inspection may be just the right time for you to do a 'cavity search.' By now she may already be dripping in anticipation. But she may also be a bit too nervous to get to the soaking stage. If she's not wet enough for a cavity search, lube your fingers with the water-based lubricant of her preference. Never, ever use things like oils, butter, lotion or other goo not intended for pussy consumption. If you don't have proper personal lubricants, use spit. How nasty and sexy! You've got plenty. Better yet, make her lick your fingers until they're dripping. Your cavity search should begin slowly, methodically and thoroughly. Keep her in suspense. Slowly speed up. The next part may be a bit counter-intuitive for men. Make her come. Don't use your dick, but use your fingers, hand, tongue, vibrator or what ever it takes to get her off. I have found that women are generally more sexually sensitive and receptive after one good orgasm. Guys, trust me on this one. Subsequently she'll process teasing, pain and torment more sexually than before that righteous come. Just consider this as priming the pump.

On one occasion with a playmate named Candi I used a deluxe deep penetrating twisting vibrator with a vibrating clit stimulator. I combined the toy fucking with manipulating her clit shaft with my fingers. I could feel her little bud swell between my thumb and forefinger. I let the pleasure linger. I teased her with the vibrator mercilessly, keeping her at the edge of orgasm until she was begging for it. After sufficient suffering I let her have one good long shudder. Driving home the point that I can pleasure her…. If I want to.

Some women find that they get a lot more sensitive after their pube hair is gone. Some women prefer to get professionally waxed, others like the intimacy of a shave from a partner. If so, shave her. I personally prefer to shave with a disposable straight razor. For some reason my subjects are much less fussy and better behaved when I'm wielding a straight razor over them. Since I'm a sadist, sometimes I chose to use a

106

menthol based shaving cream, but I wouldn't' recommend this if this is new to you or your bottom's not a pain pig. Candi had tried really hard not to squirm with the menthol while I shaved her. She couldn't hide her excitement, however. Not all the lubrication for the shaving was from the can. Her cunt was dripping. Wash and dry your subject off well. Hand held shower massagers can provide nice to nasty sensations on her cunt. Then proceed to enjoy the smooth naked skin.

Once the pussy's excited, the whole area is engorged with blood and becomes more sensitive to temperature change than before. Play with hot and cold sensations. Ice is a great toy. You can use regular ice cubes or make ice dildos using popsicle forms. Don't ever use actual ice pops or frozen desserts of any sort. She'll hate you when she gets a yeast infection from that stupid move. I have used a glass full of regular ice cubes and slowly teased Candi's outer lips, the valley between her lips, her inner lips, her clit hood and then her opening. Cube by cube I stuffed her cunt full of ice. Then I pulled her clit hood back, exposing fully her swollen clit, and slowly and precisely dripped warm water onto it. (Warm water only, please. It's a bad idea to use scalding hot water.)

Certain substances give a hot or cold sensation without actually being hot or cold. Many muscle creams have a hot-cold sensation to them, like Ben Gay or IcyHot. I like Tiger Balm. It's pretty obvious what these creams can do to the skin. Use it only on the outside. They're not meant for internal use. If you're going to play with any of these sorts of goo, start with a very small amount. Make sure to have some witch hazel, mild skin lotion, wet towel and aloe vera gel near you as well. Once the intensity gets too much you must neutralize the effect of the substances immediately. Witch hazel will cut oil-based material. Lotions will neutralize them. The wet towel will remove it all and the aloe will help soothe the skin. Before playing, it might be a good idea to patch test the goo on regular skin, such as her thigh, to make sure that she doesn't have allergic reactions to it.

There are other fun tricks as well. Some times I like to enjoy sushi in a very creative and particularly Japanese way. A little sushi and wasabi for me, a little wasabi for Candi's cunt. There was one occasion when I reached under the table at a sushi restaurant with a finger full of wasabi and shoved it well and deep into her pussy and went on our way, and I watch her squirm with each step. Breath fresheners are great too. Take a mint candy in your mouth and go down on her and watch her jump! Those little bottles of liquid breath freshener drops work wonders

107

on clits and cunts. I have found that the cinnamon flavored ones are particularly effective. A wiz in the kitchen? Take a fresh ginger root, peel off the skin and place the ginger on her outside skin. Is she a masochist? Try inserting the ginger plug. A few words of very real caution. Don't use chili oil or hot sauce. These oils can blister her tender skin. Once she's been blistered, she'll probably never want you to have anything to do with her cunt ever again.

Now that the skin is all naked, sensitive and aroused, go to the bathroom cabinet and bring out the electric toothbrush. A sadistic dentist, I am convinced, invented the electric toothbrush. It's the best little torture tool to amp up the erotic anguish. It's great on nipples and cocks, but it's fantastic on cunts. Begin from the outside of the pussy and slowly work your way towards the bull's eye of the clit. The anticipation of the sudden shock to the poor abused clit alone will drive her out of her mind! If you use it on any regular basis she'll shudder and soak herself just by hearing its unique buzzing sound. The electric toothbrush is just the beginning. Collect all sorts of brushes for your nefarious purposes. There are water pick style power toothbrushes, and regular toothbrushes from baby soft to mercilessly firm. Baby hairbrushes, paintbrushes, make-up brushes, dog and cat grooming brushes, nailbrushes, mushroom brushes.... Etc etc. You get the picture. Alternating between a sensually soft strokes to the cruel rasp of a harsh brush will also keep her head spinning and you in cuntrol. I'm sure Mr. Fuller's wife was a very happy woman.

After raiding the bathroom cabinet, now go to the office drawer and the laundry area. Gather all the different kinds of clips that you can find. Plain wooden clothespins are classic essentials of cunt play. Other types of clips are great too; plastic clothes pins, memo clips, metal file clips and even hair clips. The most evil type of clip I've ever used was (now, sit down before you read the rest of this).... Hello Kitty paper clips. They have evil little plastic teeth that slowly grip deeper and deeper into the labia. What can I say, I'm sick. I like the sadist's humor of using a cute pussy logo clip to torture a willing pussy. Remember that each cunt is custom designed. Places to clip will vary from cunt to cunt. Find where you can pinch up a good deal of flesh and then clamp on a clothespin. Don't just pinch a thin layer of skin with the tip of the clip. That usually hurts in a very non-erotic way. Line the labia with lots of clips. Get decorative. Pretend you're a pervert Martha Stewart. (I do. Does this make me the Martha Stewart of Kink?) You can even use a clip on the clit hood if you're careful. Not many people can take a clip directly on the clit. Don't push it. After you leave the clip on for a while, pick one up and shift it over a half an inch. Do the same for all of them. Re-decorate. The rush of blood to the crimped skin juxtaposed with the new clamping will drive her wild! This is called 'walking' the clips. Nipple clamps are good as cunt clips too. Tiny plastic vices and spreader tools used for model making work well also.

Percussive play is a must for pussies. Percussive play is any sort of play that involves a striking motion. Small rubber whips that look like key chains are perfect for cunt whipping. Try different striking methods and implements. Good old-fashioned spanking directly on the cunt can make girls like my friend Candi to go wild. Be careful, or you might end up with a drenched hand by the time you're done swatting her pink bits.

You'll be surprised as to all the creative implements are around you. One night I ordered Candi to drop her panties and sit in the kitchen sink after she finished the dishes. I took the rinse nozzle hose and played with the pressure and temperature on her excited vulva. Her whimpering was music to my ears! A suction cup with a pump handle, typically used for nipples is a great way to force attention from a clit and it's possessor. Pump it up, remove the hose and tease her swollen member. Flick the cup with your finger. Put a vibrator on it.

Want to get advanced with this stuff? Combine them. Change the pace. Enjoy yourself. There are other advanced play styles like fisting, piercing, catheters, suturing and electrical play, but we'll leave that for another time.

So now that you know a few new tricks, watch her go out of her mind. Out of her mind and in to your cuntrol. That's just how we like it, isn't it? So now, what are you going to do with for the rest of the evening?

Go out and have some fun! Remember to have great sexy time and always play safely.

Pleasures of Rope Bondage, for Beginners

Have you ever had a lover's caress that lingers for hours and hours and strokes every contour of your body?

Have you ever held your lover in an embrace that's all encompassing?

Have you ever felt the total abandon of mind-bending, body shattering orgasm while safely contained so as to keep you from shattering away into nothingness?

Have you ever felt the magic and power of being a sexual alchemist creating unsurpassed pleasure for your lover?

If you've felt these, you know the magic and pleasure of rope bondage.

Bringing this pleasure into your bedroom isn't difficult. Sure, those hot photos you see in fancy Japanese bondage books and on-line bondage sites may seem intimidating, but rope bondage in real life doesn't have to be. Rope bondage can be fun, easy and most of all extremely sexy. Now, let's try introducing some sexy bondage games into your bedroom escapades. You'd be surprised as to just how many people enjoy a little bound kink from time to time. No need to get super complicated. You don't need to have special equipment or Eagle Scout knot tying know-how.

Here's what you need:

First you need a willing partner in pleasure. Sweetly ask your lover if he or she might enjoy a light bit of bound fantasy along with their favorite sex play. Keep it fun and light. You don't want to scare your lover into thinking that you've suddenly turned into some freakazoid. If they seem a bit hesitant, you might want to remind them that you simply want to make them happy. If they're hot and revved already, well, then go on to the next step.

Get yourself a blindfold or a scarf. Sometimes this is all you need to get that spicy fantasy going. It can be as simple as a scarf or as fancy as a fleece padded locking leather blindfold. Make sure to not tie it too tightly around the head, especially if your lover wears contacts. If you want an unusual, cheap and medically inspired alternative, consider a self-adhering eye bandage patch.

Now you need to get rope. There are many kinds of rope to get. I really like cotton rope, but it can be hard to find. Try the thicker cotton sash cords from the hardware store or magician's rope available at magic stores by the spool. These kinds of rope are soft, and they get softer with use and washing. I also find that upholstery cords available at fabric shops are nice because they're soft, sensual and pretty. Hardware stores are fantastic, as are marine supply stores for nylon and polypropylene rope. Climbing rope is not too friendly on the skin, so I'd leave that out. Hemp rope can be very seductive for Japanese bondage enthusiasts, but it is more difficult to come by, especially in the pre-conditioned, soft Japanese style. It's good to have many different thicknesses, textures and weaves. Experiment with various types and see what you like. While there's no strict guideline, you'll want to have many different lengths of ropes. Try having several skeins of rope at 25 to 30 feet, some at 10 to 15 feet and even a few that are 6 to 8 feet. If you get rope that's much longer than 30 feet, it becomes bulky and harder to handle. You end up wasting more time on handling the rope than binding or playing with your lover. Keep your ropes short. You can always add more.

Attachment points are nice to have for bedroom rope bondage enthusiasts. Four-poster beds and beds with headboards are great for adventurous lovers. Before your hot bondage date, attach thick ropes to the headboard. Make them the length to where they'll reach extended arms and legs, plus 3 feet or so. With this you can swiftly tie in your pleasure slave into position for consensual ravishing without any awkward fumbling. If you don't have a bondage-friendly headboard, you can run two lengths of rope under the mattress or futon that's long enough to reach the arms and legs. When it's not playtime, all you need to do is tuck the ends under so your bedroom can look as chaste as a saint's!

Don't forget the "Safe Word" or "Safe Signal." This is the simple word or body signal that the two of you agree to mean, "no, really stop." This way you can have all of the fantasy struggle and even say 'No!' that really means "no, don't you dare stop the amazing thing you're doing to me!" Another item to have on hand is a pair of safety shears: A blunt end, all purpose pair of scissors so you can cut the ropes if necessary. Rope cutters for climbers are also good and easy to use. This is just in case you realize that the earth is REALLY moving and it's not just because of that great orgasm. I don't ever like to leave this particular item out... After all, I do live in earthquake country, here in California.

Now take some rope, lay your honey down comfortably and caress her with the rope. Just let it slowly drape across her body as if the ropes were your hands and fingers. This can be so sensual and mesmerizing that she'll be purring in no time!

Start out by looping the rope around her wrists and ankles loosely and tying it off with a simple square knot. Do the same with her ankles. This gives her a sense of what rope bondage feels like, something to hold on to, yet with the assurance, at this early stage, that you can bring her easily out of it. It'll also give you the chance to get familiar with basic rope combined with good sex to equal a great time.

You got this down? Great! Go and pick up a Boy Scout manual on knots and ropes. That's a great guide. For more information on safety stuff, check out Jay Wiseman's *Erotic Bondage Handbook*. If you want to get more into the sensual psychology of bondage and Japanese rope styles, check out my book *Seductive Art of Japanese Bondage*.

Why does rope turn me on so much? Why do I love rope bondage so dearly? To me, the rope is an extension of my arms, fingers, legs, lips and tongue. I may have only two arms to embrace you with, but I have miles of rope to wrap around you. The rope becomes an extension of my desire for you... Sometimes it caresses you softly and sensually. Wrapping the rope around you like the delicate silk of a cocoon, I protect you from the harsh world. Sometimes I am feeling the cruel desire to sink my teeth and talons into your flesh. Then the ropes will dig into your skin, letting you feel my hunger to possess and devour you. My desire is so entwined with the rope that I can feel your every twist, turn and struggle against the rope as if it were against me.

Bondage is also an act in which beauty is created between two people. When I bind, I make certain that I frame the woman in such a way as to bring forth her beauty, grace and sweet vulnerability. When I bind,

112

I make certain that I show the man's strength, power, handsomeness and seductive sensuality. The bottom to me becomes like the living flower and trees in Japanese flower arrangement or tree sculpting. Their natural beauty, creativity in motion and grace in body-awareness combine with my craft and art to create a collaborative work of movement and restriction – the body natural and the body redefined.

Over the years, I have enjoyed many hot bondage scenes with some remarkable beauties and have even shot the results with some talented photographers. When I create bound body art for stage and photography, each woman and man is an exotic flower to be framed.... I find features of their body that I wish to emphasize... large emotive eyes, beautiful feet, voluptuous breasts, the sensual curve of a strong back, etc... and then I bind them in a way such that their beautiful is sensuously strained and emphasized with grace.

Creating beauty and art is a sex act for me. There is no higher pleasure for me than combining all my senses with another to create something that moves me in all parts of my brain – and moves me to the core of my body as well.

Measure of a Perv

If a leatherwoman doesn't play for a long period of time, is she still a leatherwoman?
If a leatherman chooses SM abstinence is he still Leather?
If a kinkster doesn't play for a long time, are they still a kinkster?

Yes, Virginia, you're still a pervert!

> *This is dedicated to a dear friend of mine who's been wondering if his license as a perv has an expiration date.... And to all who've retreated from kink and leather in their time.*

We must understand that pleasure can't be rushed or forced. That would be like flower blooming in a false early spring. It could end up damaging the plant's longevity. Pushing to play may have negative consequences in the long run. At times our pleasures lie dormant like bulbs waiting for the warm rays of spring.

The dedication or orientation of a perv or a leather folk is not merely measured by her quantity or duration of play. It's not even measured by how hard she plays. Rather, it's a combination, in varying formulation from person to person, of sexual self-awareness, principles of personal relationships, natural or nurtured sexual orientation towards kink, philosophy of living, social activity, community involvement, practice and play.

Even if a person doesn't play for a long stretch of time, she's still a pervert. I believe that my desire for SM, D/s and fetish is hard wired into me. It's my orientation, just as much as queerness, heterosexuality and bisexuality are orientations for others. I maybe active or inactive, or I may even (gasp!) engage in "vanilla" sex, but that doesn't change my orientation as a perv. It's like this: a heterosexual man is still heterosexual even if he's celibate. A gay man can play with a lesbian but their orientations are not changed. I simply know and accept that kink is part of my orientation. As an orientation, it's not something that disappears due to inactivity.

Living the leather life is also defined for many by the forms of relationships consciously entered into, not by the frequency of SM scenes in their lives. I have chosen to place most of my erotic or intimate relationships in the framework of D/s. I'm also dedicated to getting off with kinky sex. My preference is kinky sex over vanilla sex. I have chosen to be out as a perv. I have chosen to be an active member of the kink community locally, and beyond. I consciously strive to learn more about my SM skills and in turn to learn more about myself through SM. I work and live in a way that I can be honest to my kink orientation. I have based many of my life decisions and a personal philosophy for my life around this orientation. That's a commitment. It's a commitment that is no less valid whether I play SM every night, once a month or once a year.

Sometimes my desire for kinky play lowers because I'm busy, distracted or under the weather physically or emotionally. This passes when my schedule clears or I return to good health, and hot play ensues. Sometimes the desire might wane because I've entered a contemplative phase around SM. Sometimes this is burnout and other times this is a period of re-evaluation of my own desires. Then when I emerge from a period of self imposed exile I play with renewed ferocity, whether that reemergence takes the shape of private play only or extends to public play. There have even been times where disappointments or disillusionment in the leather/SM/fetish community led me to rein in my play. In such situations, some catalyst has always come around to restore my faith in the leather community and kink life.

Such a restoration of faith in pervery happened for me once in Salt Lake City. Yes, in that bastion of conservative Mormonism, I raised my hand to leather and cried "Hallelujah!" I'll admit it, at that time I had been experiencing a few issues that made me a bit sad about trends I'd noticed in the kink world.... On the other hand, maybe I was just getting crotchety in my "old" age. (Bitter old queens come in many ages and shapes, after all!) I'd been feeling a bit like the sexy sizzle in SM play and community had been fading, suffocated under the sheer size of the community and bureaucratization of pleasure. I've been to events where it felt more like I was at a trade convention for widgets in a clean, well lit hall rather than the gathering of hungry pervs. The lights are brighter and the streets are cleaner in the Meat Packing District of New York and South of Market in San Francisco. Play parties smell more of antiseptic surface cleaners than sweat, blood and cum. This may simply be part of the social evolution of the community, but it does dampen my leather lust. I found myself wondering, "What's going on here?"

In the midst of such doubt, however, I was invited to Salt Lake City to teach an intensive weekend program to a private SM academy where men and women, regardless of orientation, top or bottom, enter into a 12 to 18 month education on leather, SM, self awareness, community building and spirituality. The academy leader and cadre turned over their freshmen class to me for the entire weekend to train them as I wished. I put them through what I can basically describe as Midori's Leather Boot Camp. Using unorthodox methods I pushed them physically and emotionally while doing a mass brain dump of SM info from my head to theirs. They rose to the challenge, kept up with me and showed me passion, compassion and drive. They learned well and in so doing thrilled me as a teacher. Teaching them let me return to my beginner heart and reminded me how thrilling it is to live true to my desire in the leather life and that passion still burns in the community.

I think I'll be lining up some hot SM play between my hurricane paced travel schedule!

So, dear friend, your perv license has no expiration date. Only you can surrender that identity.

Visiting San Francisco for a Wild Weekend?
or
How to Look Cool while Hanging with Hardcore Perverts

Welcome to Sodom, Dorothy! You're not in Kansas anymore.

This is your chance to go to a kinky club, a SM dungeon or a fetish fete. Contrary to popular fantasy, however, it's a world that has it's own code of conduct. Screw it up and not only will you not get to screw, but also you'll get bounced out of the door and blacklisted by the bouncer or organizer.

Here are some tips to help you get in the door, be cool and maximize your cruising potential.

First, you want to find out what the expected dress code for each part of the wild weekend is. At fetish nightclubs you can wear outrageous clothes but usually the naughty bits need to be covered. At a dungeon play party where it's mainly about SM play, you can usually, but not always, let it all hang out. If there are SM workshops, then you can dress more casually. You don't have to drop a fortune on new duds, but the more you adhere to the dress code, the more likely you'll be greeted as part of fellow freakdom. Dress to fit in and more people will want to have fun with you. Dress like a tourist gawker and you'll be ignored.

Second, never touch anyone or anything without the person's (or the item's owner's) explicit consent. Yes, that hot stranger, the babe with the ass and tits hanging out, suspended from the ceiling like a ripe piece of fruit ready for the picking may look touchable and inviting. Don't touch! She's not your date or your slave. She didn't agree to play with you, she's only consented to being voyeured by others. Uninvited touch is the fastest way to get 86-ed from the club.

Third, meet lots of new people, introduce your self with a smile and explain that it's your first time. Veteran kinksters just love to show enthusiastic, polite newbies around. You'll get lots of insider information from them such as where the private parties are. Sexual community locals love to help an honest 'virgin' but really dislike dealing with 'posers' who pretend to know things when they don't.

Fourth, don't chat loudly in dungeons and sex parties. It's distracting and considered rude to talk in a dungeon play space or sexual arenas. Remember not to make negative comments about other people's scenes or encounters regardless of how scary or creepy they may be to you. You think an enema's gross? You're scared of a double penetration suspension scene? Hey, you may be doing that very thing a few months from now. I've heard it said that in the SM scene "I'll never..." means about 6 months!

Lastly, if you don't know how a local event or group does things, ask the organizers for their advice. They'll be helpful, as they want you to have a good time too!

Looking for Kink Clubs?
For a thorough listing in each state and major cities in the USA see http://www.darkheart.com/sceneusa.html and the Leather Journal Web site at http://www.theleatherjournal.com/directory.htm

Age limits may apply with many of these organizations.

Midori's Quiz: "Is Your Prospect A Proper Pervert?"

To finish this section on a lighter note, here's a quiz I published just when spring fever was hitting us in 1997!

The smell of leather and pheromones have been wafting in the air recently as yet another spring approaches, our brains turn into scrambled eggs as our loins take over our rational, highly developed decision making abilities. We turn into leather-clad apes in heat. But BEWARE, pervy readers! You don't want to end up bringing your latest, greatest victim - err I mean trick - home only to discover that he or she donates to the religious right, anti-porn movement. So, let the Fetish Diva give you a hand! Cut out the Perv-Screener Test below and stow it in your leathers with the condoms and ask them these questions. (Preferably before exchanging saliva, although exchanging names may be optional.)

1. Where would you want to go for a first date?
    a. A nice movie at the local Cineplex
    b. Jaguar Books (men's sex toy shop) or Good Vibrations (women's and couples sex toy shop)
    c. Nob Hill Cinema (gay strip joint and sex club) or the Lusty Lady (peep show with hot women)
    d. A poultry market

2. Which of the following movies or shows make you hot/hard/horny/wet?
    a. *Kama Sutra* or *Queer as Folk*
    b. *9 1/2 Weeks*, *Cruising* or *Deep Throat*
    c. *Blood Sisters* or *Gladiator*
    d. *Little Mermaid* or *Sordid Lives*

3. What's your favorite underwear?
   a. Victoria's Secret or Calvin Klein
   b. Rubber panties or a latex jock
   c. Locking leather chastity device with a spiked cod piece
   d. Live chicken

4. For foreplay, you like
   a. Long walks on the beach
   b. Silk scarves for blindfolds
   c. A trip to Mr. S Leather or Madame S Leather
   d. Poultry

5. You have a fetish for
   a. What's a fetish?
   b. High heels and Cuban heeled stockings or police boots
   c. Latex catsuits
   d. Chicken feathers

6. Your favorite female sex symbol is...
   a. Britney Spears
   b. Betty Page
   c. Grace Jones
   d. Big Bird in drag

7. Your favorite sex act
   a. Missionary in your bed with the lights out
   b. Doggy style with a rubber toy
   c. Mummification with plastic wrap and liquid latex
   d. Two hands and a carton of Grade A Large

8. Which would be your favorite sexual setting?
   a. Martha Stewart Living bedroom set with the lights out
   b. Ménage à trois on black satin sheets
   c. A hot evening with a stranger at a sex club
   d. Midnight rendezvous at Foster Farms

9. "SM" means...
   a. San Mateo county public transit
   b. Sensual Magic
   c. Sado-Masochism
   d. Stuffed with Mushrooms

10. Your favorite bedtime reading includes...
    a. *Reader's Digest* Magazine
    b. *Lady Chatterley's Lover, Playboy* or *Playgirl*
    c. *Macho-Sluts, Master Han's Daughter* or *Bound & Gagged*
    d. *365 Days Chicken Dinners*

Fetish Diva Midori's fabulous pervo-decoder:
Add up the points for each question as follows:
    a=1, b=2, c=5, d=10

If your prospect scored from 10 to 15: Encourage them to join a convent or the priesthood. They'll get more action there.

If your prospect scored from 16 to 25: Fresh, eager and clueless... Break them in slowly and you'll be their sexual deity for life. Either that or they'll turn you in to the authorities.

If your prospect scored from 26 to 35: Perv poster-babe! Probably dated half of your exes.

If your prospect scored from 35 to 45: Kink dynamo! They may wear you out, but you'll die a happy perv! I hope you have two weeks' supply of lube.

If your prospect scored 46 or above: You have two choices. Turn and run or take a month off work and don't expect to walk normally ever again. Can you squawk like a chicken?

Part Three: Fetish Eroticism

Photo by Steve Diet Goedde

Fetish vs. SM/Kink Explained

Ever notice that anything to do with adventurous sex and alternative sexuality gets all lumped together? Fetish, SM, Kink and Leather – they're all bundled together as if the people, action and words were totally interchangeable. We expect this sort of simple assumptions from media and Joe-Public. But this phenomenon also happens among those of us in these very subcultures that enjoy these sex styles. You'd think, of all people, we would know better. Many of us use words, phrases and cultural references interchangeably, without consideration for the actual distinctions between them.

Because all this is about sex, historically we haven't talked about the distinctions of words, actions and communities except to pathalogize the behavior. So we lack nuanced words and finesse of expression to shed light upon our pleasures. A lot of problems arise when you don't know how these terms and actions differ. If I met you at a bar and we both agreed we liked kinky sex, went home to play and discovered that you meant sadomasochistic sex with a whip while I meant fetish worship of shoes during sex – well, neither of us are going to have a good time. Let's say that a person from the Leather community met a fetishist who enjoys leather, they get together and decide to play together. When the leather fetishist discovers that the Leather community person doesn't necessarily fetishize the material of leather – and when the Leather community person discovers that the fetishist doesn't enjoy the same formal protocols – they're both going to be disappointed. They may even judge the other to be inferior in their passion compared to their own passion. It's bad enough that the general public and media bundles us all up together in blissful ignorance and self-righteousness. It's really tragic when individuals or groups of sexual minorities don't bother to understand the language, customs and vernacular of other sexual minorities.

So what's the difference? Let me share with you some quickie distinctions to get you started.

Leather community

The "Leather community" generally refers to an informal social network, mostly concentrated in North America, arising in the mid 20th century. It consists generally of gay and lesbians who enjoy sadomasochistic sex and put value on organization and hierarchy in their personal social relationship. You'll find writings by Dr. Gayle Rubin, Joseph Bean and Jack Rinella helpful for this. Also check out the books *Urban Aboriginals* and *Leatherfolk*. Curiously a person may identify that they are a "Leatherman" or a "Leatherwoman" but may or may not have a fetish for leather. They may not even be into heavy SM but feel that they are part of a community. So the term really focuses on one's social affiliation, rather then a focus on a particular sexual practice.

Kink

Kink is a really general term covering all sorts of "unusual sex." According to Dr. Robert Bienvenu, a sociologist who studies sexual minorities, "kink" is a term indigenous to those who practice it. It's not a word that doctors created to indicate a disorder. Any one can be kinky or identify as kinky, regardless of age, gender, orientation or social affiliation. There are plenty of people who are kinky who don't belong to some kinky social network.

Sadomasochism

SM, or sadomasochism, generally refers to those who like to play with intense sensation. When the terms "SM community" or "BDSM community" is used, it often refers to an informal social network of those who enjoy kinky sex. The term is used over a larger population base, including more pansexual and heterosexual kink practitioners. The use of "BDSM" became more popular with the Internet. Those who identify as part of the SM or BDSM community don't always share the values and rituals of the Leather community.

Fetish

"Fetish" and the "Fetishists" are another different category. The loose social network of fetishists seemed to have started earlier then the Leather community and tends to be more heterosexual. Dr. Bienvenue has written extensively on the 20th century Fetish communities. Individual fetishists, however, exist among all sorts of people. Many consider themselves in varying ways to be kinky, or feel they belong to the Leather community, or identify with the BDSM community. Some feel so affinity with any groups.

I know a bit about the fetishists, as I am one. But I'm also kinky with affiliations with the BDSM, Leather and Fetish communities.

So what's a fetishist? Let me explain...

Fetishists Explained

The dark seductive smell of leather sends a rush of adrenaline into my chest. I am aroused.

In the tight shiny second skin of latex, my curves slide through the world, a flesh-made high performance super racer. I feel sleek and sexy.

Snug leather gloves encasing my delicate hands drop me into a narcissistic swoon with each tightness-amplified pulse. I am turned on.

The bold architecture of stiletto heels mesmerizes me, whether I stand atop six-inch pedestals or gaze upon them, covetously, in a couture shoe shop. My libido flares.

The raw smell of industry, progress and war permeates my nostrils in the black gas mask of thick rubber. I dream of recreating the self into machine flesh of sex and death. I am excited.

Encased in animal sensuality and inhaling the musky, primal scent of fur, I wallow and purr, like a saber-toothed cub in a prehistoric mother cat's den, feeling carnivorous power just beneath my thin skin of humanity. I am wet.

In short, I am a fetishist.

I am also a sexual dominant in the D/s realm as well as a SM switch and bondage lover. Contrary to common beliefs, fetishists, SM-ers and D/s folks are not the same. They are groups of people and segments of the population that exist in overlapping circles. Some folks are limited to only a specific arena, while others have multiple and complex interests. I just happen to be sexually versatile and diversified in my interests. (Some of my friends might say that I'm just a greedy pleasure pig… and there may be a lot of truth to that, but I'll let you speculate on that.) It's easy for the world to simply lump all of the 'sexual freaks' together as one happy bunch of sick and twisted perverts. Many have joined together in socials and community spaces or in the shared spirit of the similarly marginalized. The more hostile a local community is to those who engage in "alternative sexual practices," the more closely the various pervy subgroups come together.

So what makes the fetishist unique? *A fetishist is someone whose sensual and sexual arousal is greatly enhanced by objects, body parts and other elements not directly related to intercourse.* No matter how I may try to justify it, shoes are not part of the human sexual organs and reproductive system... even if they're Blahniks. Beyond my own fetishes, which I've described above, there are loads and loads of fetishes out there. There is an infinite list of potential objects that may be fetishized by someone out there, bounded only by a perv's imagination. There are people who fetishize everything from A to Z: airplanes, amputees, balloons, car crashes, diapers, dressing as animal characters, guns, jock straps, Keds, long fingernails, neoprene wetsuits, stuffed animals, scars, tattoos, uniforms and X Men outfits.

Some folks are mono fetishists, dedicated in their sexual focus to one thing or a narrow range of objects grouped around a particular matter. For example, a person might find black leather riding boots to be the only thing that arouses them, or they may find the slightly broader category of men's work-boots in general, as a genre, as arousing but nothing else. Some mono fetishes may be so committed to their object of desire, so much so that any deviance (pardon the pun) from their vision of the perfect erotic object may be offensive to them or represent an abomination. Straying from their fetish ideal may possibly ruin their sexual high and sensual trance. It is as if they believe and are moved only by their one deity of pleasure.

A poly-fetishist, on the other hand, is not as specific or strict in their patterns of fetishizing the world around them. People like me, those of us who have many fetishes and the capacity to add and develop new ones, are not content in limiting our options. Sexual associations between object and pleasure seem to be made more easily among poly-fetishist, but at the same time they may lack the ritual like behavior and commitment to their objects of desires that the mono-fetishists exhibit. The rigidity of desire or behavior on the part of mono-fetishists contrasts sharply with poly-fetishists' fluid desire. To a mono-fetishist, the polys seem casual and insincere, as if they're just "playing" at being fetishists. To poly fetishists, the monos seem freakishly rigid and fearful of greater pleasures. Of course, the rest of the world simply sees both the mono and the poly fetishists as the same sexual deviants, weird and potentially incapable of "real/mature sexual intimacy."

One wonders why some people are mono and others are poly. Perhaps the mono has a greater propensity for singular love and focus, much like those who do better with monogamy rather than polyamory. Perhaps the poly folks are sensualists or more hedonistic, looking for the next new thrill. Perhaps both varieties have the propensity towards fetishism but the mono fetishist had a singular and momentous imprinting event early in their development where the poly fetishist did not. Who knows? I'm just speculating here. Unfortunately I don't think any significant research money will be going into solving this mystery any time soon.

Fetishism seems to span demographics. Fetishists reside among all sexual orientations, gender identifications, classes, races and cultures. It's worth noting, though, that research seems to indicate there are more cases of guys than gals who are fetishists. I wonder if that's the wiring or the socialization of sexual permission? As for cultural variation, some cultures seem more tolerant of particular fetishes than others. Augmented large breasts are fetishized by many in the United States, much like sailor style school uniforms are in Japan and bound feet were in not-so-long-ago China. Some communities and cultures may also be very negative about particular fetishes, while accepting of others. Having a breast augmentation is acceptable, and liking it is certainly acceptable in the US, yet foot binding isn't. The scars of a history of racism, slavery and segregation create reluctance and hostility in many communities against particular fetishisms as well. Fetters and collars do not go over well for the African American communities. "Yellow Fever" (the fetish for and objectification of Asian people as a group) isn't much appreciated by Asians. Play with Nazi uniforms among certain circles? Take a guess how well that would be accepted. Yet even among these and other communities with their own taboos on fetish sex, there are people who engage in exactly those forms of fetish sex play.

While fetish inclinations seem to arise among all groups of people, different economic and class level affects the access to material, sexually tolerant environment and much needed privacy to engage in alternative sex. Simply put, if you're rich, white, and single, you can buy the fur, leather or latex, have the home and personal space to enjoy it in, fly to places to meet other like-minded fetishists and the money to pay legal fees if you're busted for violating some local decency law and not catch grief from your people while you're at it. If you're poor, you have to spend your resources on survival, not kinky pursuits.

This may be one of the factors around why it seems that fetish sex play belongs to the white, middle class and higher socio- economic groups.

Unlike D/s, fetishism at its purest form is not about power exchange and can be enjoyed in the absence of power exchange. A fetishist can play as a top, a bottom or, (gasp!) an equal. It's a common misconception that a fetish worshipper must be a bottom. The bottom worshipping the boots on her mistress' legs isn't the only fetishist in the room. Unlike most sadomasochists, a fetishist may not even need another person to enjoy the sensuality of their focal object. I can have a perfectly wonderful and mesmerizing erotic time, alone with a pair of gloves and a fur coat, thank you very much! A fetishist may also engage in very "vanilla" sex, unlike their SM compatriots. If someone is dressed in thigh-boots and a crotchless latex cat suit, even the most mundane missionary-style-with-the-lights-out sex becomes wildly kinky – even though, strictly speaking, it's still "vanilla" by SM and D/s standards.

This may explain why some SM and D/s players see the fetishist as "light weight," as not "serious" or simply as "tourists" among true sexual adventurers. They measure kinkiness by degree of SM or D/s present, in other words, by their own yardstick, and fail to recognize the fundamental nature of the motivations, turn-ons and behavior of the fetishist. Many SM and D/s players are themselves fetishists. For them, the fetish is intertwined with other aspects of their sexuality. Therefore it may be difficult for them to relate to the fetish purists who have no need for power or intense sensations in their sex lives. It is interesting, however, that there seems to be a higher rate of SM/Ds players who have fetish interest than the general population. Why? Maybe they are simply using the fetishistic attire as a community uniform. Maybe there is an overlap in the ability to experience sex symbolically for those who get turned on by a flogging and those who get turned on by leather. Maybe they're just not satisfied with limited sexual expression acceptable to the main stream – perhaps they are both restless and creative sexual explorers.

How about you?

Fetishism: Sex, Romance and Ritual:

The intoxicating heady scent of fine leather fills my nostrils as a pair of exquisite vintage gloves slides out of their ancient cellophane wrapper into my hands. The supple leather seems warm to the touch. The deep blue-black color and its delicate thin skin transfixes me. I smell, caress and admire them with reverence before I peel apart the opening and slide smoothly into them. The inner skin is soft as silk velvet. The gloves embrace me and mold warmly to me as if they had been waiting for just this moment. A perfect fit?! Yes! I'm delighted. Nearly to the elbow, they embrace the soft swelling of my forearm. Feeling as though caressed by an old lover, I sensuously run my hands over each other I savor the sensation alone. It feels right. It feels sexy. I feel a familiar power surge through me. My heart beats a bit faster.

Sensing another heart beating faster, I look over to my boi servant. She's a bit flushed. With her eyes wide and her pupils dilated, anticipation fills her face. Still, she knows her place and proper behavior. She sits quietly; a precarious yet practiced balance of desire, loyalty and focus. I reach my glove-encased hand out towards her.

"Ma'am, no... please..." Soft pleading voice escapes her lips. A final and futile effort to maintain composure, before certain meltdown of any remaining

shred of composure. Leather fingers caress the hollow in the nape of her neck. She shudders and leans ever so slightly back into my palm. With a gentle pressure I pull her towards me. She yields to the touch of the gloves and to my desire. Her head now in my lap, she curls into a fetal position. Stroking her face I let her take in the scent of the hide. She moans. I cover her face with my hands, taking over her thoughts. She gasps. I slide a finger between her lips, penetrating her being. She shudders deeply.

My heart is filled with affection.... A affection peculiar to dominance and submission. My sex throbs with excitement... A lust peculiar to fetishists.

Lately my mind has been pondering fetishism - that powerful erotic association of material goods or body parts not essential to intercourse and enhanced sexual arousal.

Personally, I seem to have had a strong fetishistic inclination for most of my life. I adore tight leather gloves, lush fur and leather clothing. My fondness for uniforms certainly influenced my desire to serve in the military. Fine pairs of high heels and boots mesmerize me. Having my feet or hair touched just the right way can send me into a tizzy. And then there's latex, corsets, power suits, and... You get the idea.

Sometimes I can enjoy these fetishes as solitary pleasures, but with an orientation towards erotic dominance woven deeply into the fiber of my being I prefer to enjoy them as part of SM interaction and leathersex.

Like any other forms of sex, however, mixing fetish and leathersex doesn't always work. Often after a play scene involving fetish worship I can feel very sensually satisfied. At other times I may even feel spiritually moved and feel like I am in a divine state. Yet some times I am left feeling empty and slimed with a vague sense of having been used.

It's like any other form of sex. This wide range of internal responses to seemingly identical external behavior is in part due to problems in communication and understanding individual motives. In other words, we still don't have the language and tools to express our desires. This is not surprising, given that much of society and many mental

131

health professionals still think of fetishism as a deviant, dysfunctional and unhealthy sexual expression. Granted, the social climate in parts of the world has become more tolerant towards sexual variations, but that's still not going to help the individual fetishist to safely confess his passions to his lover.

Yes, there are individuals who experience erectile or orgasmic difficulties when their particular fetish object is absent. There are a few cases where removal of their fetish object causes them to have a meltdown like a drug withdrawal. Daily functioning becomes difficult and their lives become unmanageable. This would fall under the rubric of paraphilia, according to paraphiliacs by the mental health professionals. That's not the kind of fetishist I'm talking about. The type of person I'm referring to is probably more prevalent than most think. These are the folks whose sensuality and arousal before and during a sexual encounter are enhanced or heightened by the addition of their fetish objects. Their sex life is already fun. The fetish just makes it better, sometimes profoundly better.

Even within the pervy population, fetishism can vary widely. With closer scrutiny I am sure that we can name many distinctions, subcategories and subtle variations of fetishism. Today, let me contemplate two possible distinctions. One is 'sexual fetishism' and the other is 'romantic fetishism.'

The sexual fetishist is the person for whom the object worshipped directly affects their sexual arousal. They tend to be more object focused. When I take solitary pleasure in the shape of a pair of high-heeled boots tightly wrapped around my legs, I am enjoying a state of sexual fetish.

In another example, let's assume that a stranger at a SM party politely offers to give me a sensual foot massage and worship. Let's also assume that I accept and that they're very good at such a service. The pleasure that I take from that encounter would be primarily physical and sensual, appealing to my sexual foot fetishism. The pleasure that the stranger experiences are also very likely to be focused on the delight of playing with a pretty pair of feet. We are both pleased as we are allowed to focus on our fetish objects. The relationship is secondary to the object.

The romantic fetishist is the person to whom the object worshipped is a symbolic manifestation of the underlying power dynamics of the union. They tend to be more relationally focused and their fetish is perhaps related somewhat to sexual dominance and submission.

My boy servant politely offers to give me a sensual foot massage and worship. Externally the action looks the same as when the stranger gave me a foot massage. Yet the internal experience for us is radically different. First of all, he is not a foot fetishist. He's pretty neutral about feet. He feels no more strongly about the feet than about an elbow or patch of skin on a back. Yet he is greatly aroused by this interaction involving feet. Why? Because he understood from the earliest moments of our Dominant / submissive relationship that being at my feet and providing foot service to me was a physical manifestation of our emotional dynamics. Eventually he came to associate my feet as the symbolic representation of the power that he surrendered to. My own internal experience is also more complex with romantic fetishism. Layered on top of my sexual foot fetishism and physical pleasure is the ritual acting out of our affection and chosen power relation. When my foot steps upon his face, a sense of power and deep love surges through me.

Obviously neither type of fetishism is better or worse. They're just different. Unfortunately when two people come together with mismatched expectations around fetish, the experience can sometimes result in a sense of disappointment and other unpleasant after effects.

When a person who's primarily a sexual fetishist plays with romantic fetishist, the sexually focused person might feel an unnecessary emotional burden placed upon them. Conversely, the romantic feels that their needs and humanity are being ignored and that the other is purely selfish.

While I am a sexual fetishist on my own, when I'm with others what is more important to me is the romantic fetish adoration. I know when the attention I receive is based in deep affection for who I am and in the special nature of our relationship.

I can feel passion and devotion through my boy servant's touch. At that moment alone, the world melts away around us, leaving only the two of us. The focus on each other is distilled and intensified by the rituals of SM and fetish. In a world where there is only the two of us, even in its briefness, I become divine and he, my worshipper. Over time and with the deepening of trust, these scenes become steeped in a near mystic state, where the boundary between self and other becomes thin. During the moments of ritual romantic fetish worship, the two create a space where time is irrelevant, worldly concerns meaningless and the focus is pure.

Is this what we mean by spirituality? Perhaps. Or maybe I'm just sappy. Although upon contemplation, I find it not surprising that the language of religion, spirituality, love, fetish and SM overlap.

Contemplation on Fetish And The Pursuit Of Our Objects Of Desire

As I sit in my office, which is filled with the paraphernalia of my passions and persuasions, I wonder about the power of fetish today, in this late twentieth century world. Has the power that permeated the leather of the high heel faded? Has the magic of stocking seams climbing up and under a well-fitted skirt been exorcised? Have the dark promises of supple kid gloves faded in the light of modern sensibilities?

There was a time when a Fetish was something devoutly held in one's bosom or satchel, an object of protective spiritual power from the unpredictability of fate and the harms of the world. A Fetish possessed powers very real and potent to the bearer. It seems those days are long gone in this industrialized world. You will still find Christian mystics parading saintly relics in holy places and the occasional modern day shaman in search of a material reflection of the unfathomable. But sadly, most Fetishes today are often tourist fakes lining the shelves of trendy gift and antique shops, selling off rituals to the highest bidder such that the possessor may display their fiscal potency and good taste.

One could argue that in the shift of the world from the religious to the materialistic and secular, the display and coveting of objects as symbols of power and ability to control fate is indeed the new incarnation of ancient fetish protection. Perhaps, but perhaps not. This material need to possess and display power is no different than the feudal lords of past rattling their large collections of armaments and extravagant displays of gilded trinkets for intimidation and control. The Medicis of the past are the industrial lords of today. These objects are not for protection, but rather for braggery and ego stroking.

In times more recent than when the priests of the Pueblo carried their fetishes near to their hearts, the fathers of modern psychology took the name of Fetish and called it an illness. The nineteenth century saw an unprecedented social and scientific drive to classify and organize the known universe into comprehensible compartments... whether the biological categorization of all known organisms, the classification of all known matter into the periodic table of elements or the taxonomy of the "normal" and "abnormal" minds of all humans. It is during this period of intellectual re-organization that many private expressions of passion and pleasure were deemed unhealthy and deviant. Ironically the same social climate and growth in science and industry that led to this mania for universal classification also led to the creation and empowering of objects that today are often fetishized.

The latter half of the nineteenth century found the western world in an unprecedented state of change. As science replaced religion as the key to the universe, the men of the cloth lost power to the men of reason as the bearers of all knowledge and thus authority over humanity. Social value and judgment shifted rapidly from the religious to the secular and material. The value of man, then, was no longer measured by his goodness in the eyes of a god, with a top-down yardstick. Instead worth of a man was now measured by material comforts and relative position in the eyes of his brothers, a lateral yardstick. Goodness, fulfillment, and pleasure now had material manifestations across all classes while class ascent became a new, hitherto unknown possibility. It is also around this time, after few hundred years of percolation, that the concept of the distinct and autonomous 'individual' permeates mass consciousness. With the rise of the "individual," came the rise of the concept of personal freedom in religion, thought, politics, class, destiny and private perversion.

Prior to the industrial age, the men of the cloth squelched the expression of individualism among the illiterate and agricultural masses, including individual sexual fulfillment. Reason, individuality and such were certainly pleasures enjoyed by those with privilege and resources, and likewise the ability to enjoy private sexual freedom. Social order was maintained more easily for the ruling classes with the fear of the eternal fire on their side. Social and sexual frustration was sublimated to religious fervor. Then came the industrial age and the reign of science, opening the Pandora's box to the potential of change and social upheaval. So what does this have to do with private erotic fetishes? A lot, actually, so read on.

The traditionally rural population base, of which many communities were wracked by war or famine, migrated in unprecedented numbers to the new industrial urban centers. This shift in population distribution, along with the shift of social values from the religious to the material, also had the effect of redefining the individual in relation to the community, as well as in terms of the expression of his or her own pleasure. Material things and commodity slowly became the way for individuals to directly express themselves. (You need only look in contemporary media to see today's descendants of those first solitary souls.)

The new migrants had been uprooted from religion and family and freed from the bondage of the agrarian land, and were now lost in soulless cities by economic necessity. When they felt social frustration, members of the new urban mass either acquired material goods to soothe, entertain and display their sense of individual power, as in the case of the bourgeois; or they destroyed material goods and its production to display their dissatisfaction with their powerlessness, as in the case of the early labor riots. When god was personal, people intentionally committed sins when they wanted to rebel, to show frustration. When god became a far away entity, carried off by reason and science, frustration and powerlessness turned into actions against those who seem to be the new gods, the lords of mechanization and industry – or at least, those who possessed those sources of power. When they felt sexual frustration they sought to possess the material manifestation of erotic gratification.

Naturally this newly emerging universal individualism also led to the suffrage movement - and curiously, the rising hemline. Along with that, new textile technology had made mass produced shoes and stockings available to every woman... and man. The forces of history converged upon this time and place. Individualism, materialism, societal displacement, mass production technology, suffrage and demographic realignment all set the stage for the modern erotic expression we know as fetishism. I argue that fetishism, or the erotic attraction to objects or non-reproductive body parts, cannot be solely explained through the classically psychoanalytical process of deviant infantile development. Rather, fetishism is also the individualized manifestation of internalized and sexualized contemporary societal values.

Let's consider some examples. In our society we value material power and material possessions, so when a boy comes to some sexual awareness, the materials that provocatively hide and bar his access

137

to his objects of desire, the person, eventually take on the potency of that object of desire itself. Perhaps these barriers are stockings, shoes, panties, school uniform, and for some, even veils or hajibs. Object worship in our culture is practiced widely, whether subtly or openly. Hypocritically, our culture also shuns the expressions of spiritual and sexual pursuits as somewhat barbarous; sexual expression is considered gratuitously animalistic and the fervent expression of faith is considered rather quaint.

Under these conditions it becomes easier for a boy to express arousal at the sight of an object rather than a direct sexual target. In short, if it is barbarous and undesirable to covet what is between the legs, then the shoes (a commodity considered worthy in a materialistic culture) that encase the legs are the nearest acceptable substitute to turn his desires to. Consumerism, a highly encouraged social activity is now validated as well. At an extreme, what the boy is learning is that, it's good to enjoy the Prada boots that you bought your girlfriend when she wears them but it's perverted to enjoy the legs. As a result, the act of consuming and collecting materials of mass production replaces sexual and spiritual pursuits as the road to fulfillment.

But the key to the erotic power in non-sexual objects is also the veiled element of denial and taboo. Internalized societal shame of some sort is necessary to empower these objects with the ability to arouse. I am not talking about individual shame; quite the contrary. It is my personal experience that most well developed fetishists lack a personal sense of shame in enjoying their fetish of choice. We're talking about the societal shame derived from the conflict of the individual's animal and spiritual need and the societal denial of that need in favor of material consumption. Somewhere in the conflict between individual need and societal demand, an object becomes the sublimated substitute for the animal sexual hunger.

If the individual sexually covets this object recurrently, then the animal desire, now displaced onto the object itself, becomes a subject of social scorn. This scorn, in turn increases the symbolic power of the object for both the individual and the society. Thus a simple pair of shoes can become empowered with erotic magic. So for the boy who enjoys the Pradas he bought for the girl, sublimating his desire for the legs, is now sexually aroused by the Pradas; and due to society shaming him for this desire, he now feels even more bonded to and aroused by the Pradas.

Now that we have considered one of the origins of modern erotic fetishism, let us consider the ramification of fetishism for our world today and the individual fetishists in it. Does having a fetish necessarily indicate emotional or mental dysfunction? Or rather, does it label one a hapless victim of the forces of history and society? I do not think so. After all, we humans are symbolic creatures. We interpret the world around us in sets of learned signs and communicate to one another with series of mutually agreed upon symbols called language, music and art. Sex is a form of communication, and when you think of it, human sexual expression is almost entirely a learned set of behaviors. Then it seems natural that as a reflection of the world around us, and the history before us, our sexual symbolism would include the materials that represent our objects of desire.

The catalogue of objects with potential to be fetishized is as infinite as the creativity of the human mind. The list can include; high heels, boots, corsets, gloves, stockings, pantyhose, lingerie, jock straps, masks, fur, leather, latex, PVC, silk, spandex, metal, gas mask, hair, feet, hands, legs, breasts, jewelry, tattoos, piercing, body hair, lack of body hair, cosmetics, and so forth ad infinitum.....

Other than the socio-historical background of the rise of modern fetish eroticism, what do all these objects have in common for the vast number of individual fetishists today? They have in common the power of potential. For the individual fetishist, academic reflections on the historical origins of their fetish may be entirely irrelevant. What matters to them is the promise of fulfillment, pleasure or even orgasm. The fetish object, much like the menu at a fine restaurant, give them an idea of what pleasures may come. Then the process of contemplation, desiring and waiting becomes erotic in its own languid prolonging the culmination of enjoying the fetish.

One could also say that a fetish object whispers the promise of an untold story to the lover. The seams of full fashioned stockings disappearing under a skirt point the direction towards sexual pleasure, but still nothing is explicitly revealed and the lover's desires are kept at bay. This leaves him longing for even a touch of the fetish object, the representation of the object of his desire. For many fetishists, this longing can eventually produce a dream-like euphoric state. In the end, it may be this euphoric state that the fetishist will pursue instead of the lover.

Through this rather complicated social and sexual process, the animal desire for sexual fulfillment has now been rendered into a visually triggered symbolic sensual pleasure. This sets the stage for understanding the current state of our fetish erotica. The invention of photography, film and video created a natural outlet for the pursuit of our objects of desire. The exact visual replication of these coveted objects could now be possessed and enjoyed in our privacy. The enjoyment of fetish photos and films was kept private in its early days as social pressure for sexual modesty, even of the gaze, still prevailed. As we discussed earlier, this societal pressure provided the element of shame, which then empowered these objects, and therefore the photographs were empowered with even greater potential for arousal. The symbol of a symbol was now itself the treasured source of pleasure.

Regardless of attempts to censor these fetish photographs and films from the general public, enthusiasts and those with commercial interests collaborated in creating a thriving market for fetish erotica. Some of these products are referred to as "pornographic" due to the erotic charge that surrounds them or for their original intent as sources of profit. The discussion of whether a fetish image is pornographic or not, I will leave to the readers to pursue rather than fill these pages with lengthy discourse on the topic. Let me say, however, that it has always been in the realm of the artist to take charged and evocative symbols to express himself and touch the audience in some way. And it is certainly the realm of the artist to earn a living from the worth of his or her craft and vision.

It is only natural that visual artists, especially photographers, take to fetish imagery. Individual artists may choose to incorporate fetish symbolism into their work for social, political, aesthetic or personal reasons. But the most moving of these photographs, like the objects themselves, whisper the promise of an untold story to the audience. Perhaps the difference between pornography and fetish art is the depth to which it touches the soul, whether the viewer is a fetishist or not.

But in more recent times, has the magic of fetish begun to wane in the West? The social climates in America and Western Europe during the second half of twentieth century have slowly changed the erotic charge of fetish symbolism. The advent of the birth control pill, greater sexual freedom for both genders, and the wide availability of explicit sexual material have, at a certain level, lessened the need for sublimation of animal sexual hunger. Societal shame was shifting. Whether it's fading or not, I'm not sure. The media has fed upon this new freedom of sexual expression and upon the wider-range acceptance of the animal in us. Advertisers discovered what prostitutes and artists have always known: Sex sells. The progress of information technology in this consumerist society has flooded the market and the public consciousness with erotic and fetish images. Open any magazine today and you will find directly sexual images as well as fetishistically sexual images used to sell everything from perfume to computers. The media has filled the minds of its passive, non-interactive audience with sexual imagery from every angle. This has led to the further dilution of the power of fetish object and fetish erotica. At least, this was the state of fetish well into the 80's.

The past couple of decades, however, have seen a new increase in interests towards fetish. Two major reasons contribute to this. The first reason is the boom in private interactive communication by way of the Internet. For the first time the consuming public could directly search for their particular fetish in the privacy of their own home. This proactivity created thriving niches for fetish enthusiasts to exchange erotic material, but also to develop new material. The second reason is the tragic pandemic of HIV/AIDS. Once again sex equaled death, although this time it was not by way of damnation from the church and burning in eternal hell-fire. No longer were we dealing with simple diseases curable by penicillin. This time, sex could result in miserable, incurable and very real physical suffering and death. Direct sexual contact was once again tainted by the fear and shame of social hysteria and suffering. These two reasons set the stage for today's rebirth of fetish erotica.

Suddenly fetish was hot and sexually charged again. The consuming public now came to notice the artists and photographers who had been creating fetish erotica for years, as well as the new crop of post-HIV talents. Among these artists who have kept the fetish image alive you will the brave, often solitary, hard working, visionary, odd, and kinky people, photographers and visual artists – and certainly some of the most talented people out there. Just in terms of photographers, consider the following: Helmut Newton, Robert Mapplethorp, Bob Carlos Clarke, Irving Klaw, Marco Glaviano, Eric Kroll, Fakir Musafar, Gilles Berquet and many others of renown.

You can now add the name of Steve Diet Goedde to this list of perceptive, talented and evocative photographers. In the tradition of the greatest fetish photographers, his images are fresh and captivating. (and at this time, as I am editing this essay I find his style much copied, which also is a testimony to his talent and stylistic influence.) In his images, even the stillness of the air is full of anticipation, and they capture a sliver of a story - perhaps something very private and magical. There's often something a bit odd and unsettling about his images as well. It's not anything overt, just something strangely sensual. The viewer wonders what came before that moment and what pleasures lie ahead.... but alas, he is left wondering. Steve's photos linger in one's mind like a fragment from an erotic dream; a feeling of pleasure remains, but the details are hidden just outside our ability to fully recollect them. This is the spirit of the fetishist. The fulfillment eternally eludes them.

Steve's use of ambient light is so casual, it seems effortless. If you ask him, he may not make much of his ability to read the available light, but his talent is uncanny. The simplicity in his images is beauty. Too many would-be fetish photographers are caught up in the contrived manipulation of the object, the camera technology or the model. Steve captures a simple grace in the subject, which in turn lets the beauty of the object speak for itself.

One of Steve's blessings is his ability to draw out the magic in individual models. Having collaborated with him often, I always look forward to this process. When in front of his camera I feel an acknowledgment of a quiet grace and beauty emanating from within me. Working with Steve is a cycle of slow moments and heightened awareness, a collaborative dance with vision and body, distilled into a split-second of mutual creativity. As a model I feel free to be playful, personal, adventurous or introspective before his lens. He has a gentle affection for the subject or event before him as well as a passion for capturing the beauty and grace of the moment.

I sit in my office, surrounded by my own fetish objects and objects of desire, contemplating the modern state of fetishism. I glance up to see one of my favorite Steve Diet Goedde photos and I am reassured that the grace and power imbued in fetish symbol will not be faded by the forces of history. As a fetishist, I am encouraged.

Sex Life of Midori's Feet

As I write these words, I sit comfortably in a red velvet chair in an elegant hotel room several stories above Mid Town Manhattan. This early spring evening, the air is freshly cleansed by warm rain and cherry blossoms cover the wet pavement below. My Mac sits on my lap. I've just returned from an afternoon fetish fashion event. I'm still in my clothes from the day's festivities: a clear latex cat suit printed with cheetah spots wraps my toned flesh from ankle to neck and down to my wrists. My hands are free of my black latex gloves so I can tap away at the keyboard. The front zipper is drawn down to my waist exposing my proud and ample cleavage and my pale face is framed in a lion's mane of dark hair topped by cute little latex cat ears. My delicate feet are exposed, showing perfectly pedicured toes with Urban Decay nail polish in the shade of Bruise and one silver toe ring on the right foot. They rest upon the most perfect of footstools... a handsome naked young man lying on his back. This young man, we'll call him A, bears my collar, which he wears for his time in service to me while I'm in NYC. Around his waist winds a cord leading to intricate rope bondage restraint on his genitals. His cock and balls strain against the gentle reminder of his submission to me. My right foot rests upon the base of his cock and fully upon his tightly bound balls. My left foot presses in to his face, forcing his lips open to service my tired feet and his nostrils are firmly pressed into my arch.

This is the life.

This is the sex life of my feet.

I am a female foot hedonist. While I admire well formed feet and well turned ankles on other women, it's the pleasure of my feet and the pleasure I take in the appearance of my feet that most matters to me. I know personally that there are many of us, but we are not often spoken of or recognized. We know well of the male foot fetishists. They are numerous and their passions are catered to by many adult publications. The female foot hedonists, however, seem to be a silent, invisible or unrecognized lot. We come in many forms and many disguises. Hordes of closeted female foot hedonists go to nail salons for their weekly pedicure, to watch small Asian women pamper their commute-weary feet in mini whirlpools, scour away calluses caused by ill fitting pumps, bathe and dry their delicate unsucked toes and paint them in some color of secret passions. Other female foot hedonists are the spiritual sisters of Imelda. They cannot stay away from the latest in Guccis, Blahniks or Pradas. Their closets over flow with fanciful styles, worn only on rare occasions. Others still are self aware enough to take pleasure in an occasional toe sucking from a foot-focused lover.

Then there are the smaller numbers of feminine soldiers of fetish. We know we love our feet. The feet give us pleasure. The feet express our power as we step upon willing flesh. The feet feed the masochistic pleasures of some and bring out the secret devotions of others. The feet exist to be decorated with leather, silk and satiny fabrics. The feet propel us to new heights of ego elevation upon the pedestals of platforms and stiletto heels. The feet provide us with hidden erotic pleasures. These pleasures were well known in the court life of Imperial China, in Renaissance Venice, to the quarters of ancient Egyptian royals and in the pleasure houses of Kyoto, yet it seems all but lost and forgotten in our egalitarian modern world. Sublimated in high-tone ads from Madison Avenue and furtively lurking on the porno shelves, the pleasure life of the foot is much maligned.

Let's get back to the scene at hand. I have just covered my right foot with a couple of clear latex condoms. He's on all fours and is delightedly giving head to my foot. He knows what is to come. He pleasures it carefully, mindfully avoiding any contact with his teeth. I direct him to face the other direction and remain on all fours. I tell him to go down on his elbows and press his face into the floor. He does so obediently. A full squeeze of the lube tube prepares the target. I press gently forward. He lets out a soft moan of desire and a sigh of pride yielding to my pleasures.

If we seem to be so numerous then why are we, the female foot hedonists, the unspoken species in the menagerie of human sexuality? Is it because it doesn't sell magazines? That can't be the case since fashion and beauty magazines feature shoes and foot care... and that's a huge industry. Is it because the women are ashamed of it? Unfortunately, I don't think most women who take pleasure of their feet are aware enough to be embarrassed about their foot joys. Is it because female sexuality has been utterly discounted up until the last quarter century? Yes, I think this has much to do with it.

His moans are now deeper and more anguished. He feels my power inside of him, taking him over.

Until very recently even the importance of female arousal was ignored, orgasms dismissed, and consent was some romantic and distant notion. In a world so dismissive of basic female sexuality, how could more complicated passions of fetish and paraphilia even be considered? Our sexuality was black and white. We were either saintly chaste mothers or wanton whores. Never mind the fact that very few really knew what wanton whores *really* did much less what they personally enjoyed during their off-hours from whoredom.

What I enjoy is the pleasure given to my feet and the pleasure of power. There is nothing quite as sexy as feeling the pulse of life beneath my foot as I lay it gently on a submissive's throat. The submissive's willingness to place him or her self into such a state of vulnerability under my command sends a shiver through me that's better than the common orgasm. My feet express my passion and desires.

I desire your submission. My foot rests on your throat.
I desire your devotion. Your lips kiss my delicate arch.
I desire pleasure. My feet demand attention.

145

I desire your pain. My foot kicks your delicate parts with steel feather precision.
I desire your humility. My foot weighs down on your face.
I desire to seduce you. My foot slides up your leg.
I desire to tease you. My shoe dangles absentmindedly from a cross-legged foot.

His body begins to quiver. I can feel his muscles moving involuntarily. His mind has opened up and he invites me in fully.

Often times, sex without symbolic power inequity can be no sex at all for me. Since I'm a foot hedonist, my feet become the natural extension of my erotic power and erogenous zones. I have met other women like me. They are certainly not as numerous as the secret pedicure addicts. I know personally that there are more of us out there than you believe. Like me, these women have spent an inordinate amount of time being aware of their feet. We are transfixed by the biomechanical wonder as well as the aesthetic grace of the foot's architecture. We delight in the realization that the delicate curves of a high heel's arch echoes the curves of our own bodies.

His arms and legs quiver and he begins to slide down to the floor. With gentle firmness my foot pushes his body down into the carpet. The subtle force opens him to me even wider. His body relaxes in the assurance of the floor's support and assurance of my dominance over him.

I fondly recall one late night, years ago, with two other feet-impassioned women. N was a fully self-admitted foot hedonist and a woman who knew what she wanted. Her girlfriend, Y, a kittenish creature with a lithe body, was with us as well. This was a private evening that had begun with soaking our feet in a hot tub. Later, I had hooked N up with various electrical devices to turn her leg into a living vibrator, which I promptly planted in Y's now rather steamy crotch. In turn I planted my foot onto N's aroused sex as I spanked Y, urging her on for a better ride. And this was just the beginning of the evening!

In all the myriad of feet and leg-focused pornography, what seems to be conspicuously lacking, is the discussion from the woman's perspective. Why don't we read about the erotic tale of a woman's foot pleasures? Our world lacks the language for a woman to describe her pleasures. We owe that to the fathers of psychology - they defined any feminine tendencies to fetishism as immature sexuality and called this pathological, despite the fact that a certain level of fetish eroticism among men was accepted as normal.

> *This boy really loves my feet as well as my power through them. I can feel it in his devotion. I can see it in his dreamy expression.*

It's no wonder why men and women have such a hard time having good sex together.... I've volunteered with the San Francisco Sex Information hotline as well as other sex education outreach projects. The most commonly asked question seems to be, "how do I get my girlfriend / wife to do (insert any sexual activity here)?" or "my girlfriend / wife thinks I'm weird and sick because I like (insert any sex act other than Missionary)." When it comes to sex and pleasure it almost seems like we're speaking two different languages. Why? Because we are. The systematic dismissal of any feminine pleasures over the centuries has robbed us even of our own language of sex. Our vocabulary of lust is a poor appropriation of masculine terms for arousal or pathology. It takes a true poetess and a proudly pornographic woman to fully describe the inner pleasure of a woman's mind and body.

Without the words and names to know ourselves by, women have been forced into being deaf, blind, dumb and mute to our own desires.

> *Recovering his balance slowly, he turns around on all fours. My foot now hangs free in mid air. He caresses my foot and with the grace of a well- kept servant, liberates it from its rubbery encasement. Time moves slowly and satisfaction fills the air.*

This is why I'm out as a fetishist. I am a femme foot hedonist. I celebrate my female perversions to give name and power to my pleasures. By doing so, I force others to recognize my lusts on my terms. My uninhibited discourse about my passion for my feet and shoes may bring other sisters out of that huge shoe closet. Let's not forget, of course, that this clear identification of my pleasures and predilections makes it possible for me to get what I want in the end.

> *He's on his knees now. Looking up at me with his beautiful eyes filled with gratitude and devotion. This is the moment of peace and balance. There is nothing beyond the four walls of my temporary palace and it's just the two of us. Nothing matters at this very moment but the calm of knowing exactly who we are.*

Even as a child I had a vague and happy feeling that I was different from others. I've spent years thinking and experimenting. I have had many delusions, epiphanies and discoveries. All of this led to a conscious understanding of my sexual uniqueness. In turn this has led to my greater understanding of my whole self. I am a perv. I delight in all the flavors served up to me and then some. I'm still learning and discovering… but it sure makes my sexual quest easier when I know what my kinks are and embrace them.

When our own desires are clear, our satisfaction is inevitably within reach. Sexual self-knowledge leads to fulfilling erotic actualization as well as fulfillment as a complete person. Peace in the heart and passionate living comes from all this. You will also find that this peace and passion is infectious. Others see and feel this in you and the joy of being spreads.

So, be who you are. I guarantee it, you'll like it.

In the mean time… I'm off for a pedicure!

Allure of Femme

*She glides into a crowded room. The energy
of the room seems to shift imperceptibly. A head turns
here, a conversation stops there; the temperature seems
to rise just a bit. You can't help but notice her. There is
something quietly commanding and alluring about her.*

We've all had experiences like this. You've just encountered
that intangible effect called the Femme allure. It's the Femme Factor,
baby!

There is a mysterious power to certain women - certain Femmes.
They defy the law of physics as they raise or lower environmental
temperature by their mere presence. They confound physiology by
breaking and healing hearts with a single glance. They inspire super
human acts in those touched by them. Poets call them muses and
succubae. Some religions have damned them as witches or honored
them as magical. Hollywood of old called them Femme Fatales. Some
call them sexy, others call them wicked.

So what is this Femme allure?

You know her when you see her: Dietrich, Becall, Hepburn,
Monroe, Madonna, Cleopatra, Mata Hari, Scheherazade, Lady Murasaki,
Mary Magdalene, Madame DuBarry and so many more.

*The Femme is an icon, a fetishized idol, taking on powers
beyond her flesh-and-blood self.*

The advertising and cosmetic industry has tried to package it for generations. Lipstick and perfume come in colors called Fatale, Vixen and Glam. Although no lipstick alone can make a woman a femme fatale, a vixen or a glamour queen… Women have alternately been encouraged and cautioned against fostering those very traits within ourselves. Churches tell us it's immoral. Some old-school feminists tell women the allure is sublimated misogyny and thus demeaning. Still the women's magazines and how-to guides try to reduce it to an easily replicable formula. Remember that mid-century advice about meeting one's husband at the door wrapped in cling wrap with a martini in hand? It was supposed to keep the man's attention riveted to the wife through the prescribed creation of the dangerous siren in every Doris Day.

But formulaic advice is not enough. (Not surprisingly, cling wrap has not provided decreased divorce rates in the last few decades.) The mystery still remains as to what Femme potency is. Today, more and more women seem to seek to achieve it and look towards less conventional sources to teach them how to find power and allure in their Femme selves. At the turn of this century SM and kinky sex is the most fashionably edgy source for such information. The sexually dominant woman, as represented in SM imagery has become the current embodiment of the Femme Fatale. Unfortunately they often mistake the frills of feminine attraction for the essence of Femme power. They look for some simple explanation and paint-by-number instructions on being the empowered 'dominatrix.'

Thus, it's no surprise that every single time I teach my "Art of Feminine Dominance" anywhere in the country it's sold out. Many women attending may initially come with the idea of learning how to dominate their partners, seeking some series of techniques that will turn them instantly into confident tigresses in the bedroom. They may come seeking the panacea of kink to improve their sex lives, but soon realize that what they have been searching for is how to build the foundation towards actualizing their inner feminine power. There's a half a second of disappointment that my class does not show them how to whip, how to bind, just the right words to say to bring him to his knees. I don't do any of these. (And anyway, these are each covered more thoroughly in topic dedicated classes from many qualified sources.)

The heart of feminine potency is simple, but far from easy or formulaic. It's about confidence.

It's in a woman's confidence to know that she is a sexual being, fully deserving of pleasure and joy. In turn it's the confidence to ask without bitterness or fear for the pleasures she rightfully deserves. It's the confidence to know that she is an artful culmination of natural beauty and consciously cultivated grace. She has the confidence to know where her boundaries are and know when to change them. She knows with confidence that her weaknesses and vulnerabilities are simply elements of her totality as a powerful Femme. She embraces her vulnerabilities. They become a gift shared with those closest to her. They become the shadow that makes her fire seem to burn brighter. She is confident and knows the effect that she has on others. The alluring Femme knows that she can touch a lover's heart and soul to find strength where there was only despair. She also knows that she can destroy that very same heart and soul beyond repair. Her fire can warm the hearth as well as burn the forest down. This knowledge is the first step towards harnessing the Femme power. Those who harness it rarely seem to destroy wantonly. Those who have not acknowledged their effects leave a trail of wounded hearts and destroyed lovers.

No step-by-step instructional on female domination can teach the confidence that leads to the uniquely sexy allure of the Femme. No amount of classes on flogging and bondage techniques can create the powerful Femme. No collection of leather, corsetry, latex, boots or other fetish accessories will make a woman sexually self-actualized. These skills and adornments can serve to enhance what is already there, sometimes innately, sometimes there through lots of self-work. The accessories may peripherally help her towards greater confidence as a symbolic scepter. The strong foundation of confidence necessary to actualize the alluring Femme can only come from within her by her own efforts. Only after building for herself a strong foundation of Femme power identity and confidence can sexual dominance and Femme allure be truly effective. As I said before, the essence of Femme allure is simple, but certainly not easy to come by.

Fortunately for her, her efforts can be guided and trained quite successfully. Teachers and guides are everywhere. These are women who have struggled themselves to find their voice and power. These guides will not give a woman the formula to become the perfect dominant in the bedroom. They can, however, lead her to find her own power. They can help her from making the same mistakes they've made. This is what my teachers have done for me. I owe it to my teachers to pass on their efforts.

The aspiring power Femme will need to re-evaluate her concept of feminine power. What does she value in her own femininity? What does she feel is expected of her by her lover, her community and society at large, that in the end she can let go? What's hype and what's substance? What are her powers?

You'll find a guided exercise leading to better understanding of ones own feminine power identity in the essay "Mirror, Mirror...."

When alluring femmes and their loved ones celebrate:
Mental snapshots from my recent adventures…..

One lusty April evening in New York City, the sumptuous L'oeil Cache dungeon was entirely taken over by gorgeous leather women for one woman's very exclusive birthday play party. I swung by after a class I taught at my favorite NY sex boutique, Toys in Babeland. Old friends, lovers and friendly ex's embrace and chat, spilling out of the cozy lounge where they indulge in platters of sweets and canapés, into the elegant hallway decorated with fragrant flowers and sensual photos of dominant women. Butch, femme and andro, they're all dressed in their finest self expressive regalia: tight curve hugging custom latex, boy-ish white tank tops with well worn cargo pants, bosom enhancing corsets, latex cowboy duds, little girl cheerleader outfits, precise leatherman uniforms and more…. In one room two young butches and an evil little-girl femme ganged up on a young girlie-girl, bent her over a horse, filled every hole in every possible position with fists, dildos, toys and plugs, spanked her, pierced her and lit birthday candles stuck in the piercings. I peeked in another room and found a friend of mine having her combat boots licked clean by her sub before she precision shred her sub's back with a cruel single tail. At the other end of that room a threesome delivered a sweet cropping to a beautiful femme's creamy round bottom. Sanctity filled the air in the next room as a handsome, lean butch quietly sutured a series of semi-precious beads to the chest of her blissed-out girlfriend.

152

I cavorted and socialized, enjoying the decadence of the festivities. Later I found myself in the notorious back room, dripping in deep red and gold velvet drapings. The super-king sized, four-pillared, black-rubber-covered bed dominated the mirror-ceilinged room, lending even more elegance to the lascivious French bordello atmosphere. Or maybe it was the divinely carnal frenzy taking place on that bed that made the room seem like a wicked bordello. There, upon the enormous bed, splayed out in her ecstatically naked glory was the birthday girl. She had not a stitch on her body except a couple of dozen hungry women, obliging her birthday wish for sensual touch and sexual ecstasy. They touched, kissed, fondled, fucked, licked, nibbled, caressed, penetrated and otherwise thoroughly satisfied the woman. Many of the women pleasing her were in turn being pleased by other women, switching off and changing positions. I watched a pair of women alternately kiss each other and then go down of the birthday girl's very wet sex together. The air was thick with the smell of female sex, sounds of moans, and cries of orgasms.

New York women sure know how to celebrate a birthday!

Mirror, Mirror... How to Find the Power Femme Within

There are many of us who constantly seek the ideal Power Femme – that irresistible woman possessing the feminine allure and undeniable confidence. Our reasons are multitude. Some seek the ideal Power Femme to be a strong lover they meet eye to eye, toe to high-heeled toe. Some seek her as the echo of the universal maternal voice; the voice that reassures that all will be right and good. Others may seek her as the cool rain to calm the raging fire within their soul, or the tamer that brings the wild beast to calm contentment. Another may seek the to surrender to sweet seductions, yielding to warm, dark primal pleasures – seducing them back from intellectual civility to animal joy.

Many search for the Power Femme as their counterpart, a companion, a fulfiller of desires or a yin to their yang.

There are others still, who are not looking to her as an external 'other' or a compliment of the self. Some of us seek her, to look into her eyes and see what of ourselves are reflected in her. We seek the elements of our own spirit in her such that we may understand ourselves better and grow. We strive towards our own vision of the Power Femme.

This is all well enough in theory, but how do we come to our own vision of who we strive to be? Better yet, how do we become the Power Femme we'd like to be? These women we look towards and admire make it look so easy. Maybe they're just born that way... a human genome for Power Femme-ness. Or perhaps there's some formula for turning on the tiger-like Allure in the bedroom and the boardroom, a paint-by-number approach to Femme actualization. But really, we know well enough that neither of these can be entirely true. The former is fatalistic and the latter is far too naive.

In an earlier column we contemplated the essence of the Femme Allure. It is simple, but certainly not easily achieved. It's an artful blend of confidence and grace built upon the foundation of a conscious femme identity.

Building this solid foundation is a necessary step towards becoming our own Power Femme. In the last essay I promised you a guided exercise leading to better understanding of your own feminine power identity, which in turn will contribute towards solidifying your Femme foundation.

The Archetype

One of the easiest ways to start the process of identifying the Power Femme lurking within us is the Archetype Exercise, something I developed for the Art of Feminine Dominance class and Intensive Weekend Training.

All you need is a piece of lined paper and a pen. Now, ask yourself this question: "Who personifies the Alluring Powerful Femme for me?"

Consider categories such as myth, religion, history, family history, politics, popular culture, fictional characters as well as people in your past and present life. There are no right or wrong answers. So, go ahead and free associate! What names do you come up with? For me, names such as Catherine Denuve, Dietrich, Cat Woman, Cleopatra, Amaterasu Omikami (the Japanese sun goddess), Carmen and my grandmother come to mind. These are but a few in my list of women I admire for their Femme Allure. Now, write a name on one line, skip a few lines and write the next one, and the next one and the next one. You can do so in one sitting, or put down the list from time to time and go back to it. You may also want to bounce the question around with friends. It'll help jog your brain and remind you of such women. Others for me are the Oiran (the highest ranking courtesans of Japan), RuPaul, Emma Peel, the Nun and Drill Sergeant Rainey from my basic training.

Once you feel that you've done a pretty thorough job of listing your icons of powerful femininity, now go back to each of them. In the space after each of them write down what about them makes them Power Femmes for you. You're writing down their attributes.

155

Use words, phrases or fragments. Don't worry about the formality of structured sentences. Just brainstorm. Don't worry about whether the attributes you're writing are true or historically accurate. You need to write down your impressions of these characters, nothing more. It's purely subjective. Take for example Catherine Deneuve. I can say with confidence that she had a great sense of style. I cannot say with any certainty, however, that she felt vulnerabilities or that she understood her vulnerabilities to be part of her power. But the Deneuve that I perceive and adore in my mind does just that. So, I would write these down. This is a worksheet for you, not a clinical character assessment of these women. Some of the traits may not seem complimentary or flattering. Amaterasu Omikami was said to be fickle, Dietrich might have been selfish. Remember that the Femme is not always about 'goodness and light' or sugar and spice and everything nice. Sometimes the darker qualities of these Femmes are exactly what makes them so alluring... making them Femme Fatales. The light cannot exist without shadow. Make sure to list their attributes, the dark ones as well as the light. Do this for all the names you've listed. Then print out a duplicate or photo copy this list. Take the duplicate sheet and white out the names of the Power Femme, leaving only the traits. You now have two copies, one with the names and the traits, another with just the traits.

Once you're finished, put that list aside and go do something fun. Maybe you suddenly feel a need to find a lipstick in the most perfect shade of red. Good. Go and do it. Or maybe you have an urge to rent old Bogart movies just to lay eyes on Lauren Bacall again.

I always loved that line she uttered: "If you need me, just whistle. You know how to whistle don't you, Steve? Just put your lips together and.... Blow."

With a refreshed mind, revisit the list you made. Take the copy with the names deleted and read through the attributes remaining on the paper.

This is the dossier of your inner Power Femme. Are you surprised? It is often most difficult to see in ourselves admirable and powerful qualities. So we look at others and see, sense and project upon them what we value as femininity and power. The truth is that their traits will resonate within you. There will be a chord made of the same stuff that runs through you. These women that you admire become the landscape that echoes your own voice. Unfortunately, even in our independence- celebrating American culture women are discouraged from being self-congratulatory. Thus many women never fully develop their own image of power or accurately assess their own traits, they feel safer in admiring the power of others. A residual effect of having historically been the 'second sex' is the inability to see the strength that is within ourselves.

Recognize your personal heroines of femininity as mirrors of your own potential. This will help you to re-evaluate your concept of feminine power. How does it feel to have elements of these heroic women within you? What do you value in your own femininity?

Many Femmes may have been blocking their own potential for power due to a mismatch with externally or internally imposed expectations of feminine dominance. What do you feel is expected of you by your lover, your kink community and society at large? What have you been expecting of yourself? Are elements of Femme Power that you admire and possess as a potential within yourself conflict with these expectations? Where desires and expectations conflict, arise your discontent. Your lover thinks a sexually dominant woman should be a certain way. You act it out, it feels odd and awkward. Why? It's because your traits and desires are in conflict with his expectations. If a sexually dominant woman can't be true to herself, she's nothing but a puppet acting her way to dissatisfaction and burn out.

At any given point in play would you manifest all of these aspects of your power and personae? No. But it would serve you well to find which of these traits best describe you on a particular night of play. Do you feel demanding, neutering, coy, bitchy, precise, vulnerable, or delicate? Let the element that rings most true to you, for that moment, rule your dominant femme space. Then you'll be conducting yourself in a manner that is true to your core, not merely play-acting some externally demanded idea of what you should be like as a sexually dominant woman.

So what about the original worksheet with the names of the icons listed? Let's take a look at that. Many of the names that you listed are potential sources for role-playing for you and your partner. If Cleopatra made your list, consider the role of the imperious ancient queen. This gives you plenty of opportunity for dress up. Dressing up as characters other then your daily self may feel a bit silly at first, but it's all in the name of fun and pleasure. It will help you to create a sense of something out of the ordinary. Dress-up role-play SM games can free you from your everyday good manners and limitations. You, as your everyday self, may never imagine ordering your partner around. But you, as the queen of ancient Egypt, certainly would.

Are you're worried that your traits as a sexually dominant woman in the bedroom might carry over to your every day life in negative ways? The act of putting on and taking off the costume can give clear demarcation of when imperious behavior is appropriate and when it ends. It also gives your partner a clear delineation of when a certain type of relationship starts and ends. It's a very healthy way to create boundaries and keep playtime special and distinct from ordinary life.

Pleasure in Dressing

I am lying in bed, waiting for my lover while flipping through the latest copy of some French fashion magazine, coveting the body hugging looks, latest high-heeled boots and dangerous dresses. I'm clad in my favorite black satin push up bra, a black thong, a pair of tight black leather gloves and a pair of wickedly high black patent fetish heels. I am awash in a warm glow of sensuality as I wait for my lover. I become aware of my lover's gaze and aware of the beauty in which my personal fetish items serve to frame me in his world and the world at large. My world becomes more erotic for these sensual accouterments.

Peek into my office and you'll find me diligently working on my computer, tapping away at the keyboard towards the inevitable deadline of one article or another. Just one look at my clothing and you'll know what state of mind I'm in and the type of writing I'm doing. Am I wearing the deep green Mandarin collared pantsuit made with tightly woven, stiff cotton? That would be my "Chinese Scholar" garb and I am likely to be composing contemplative words and reflecting into the darker parts of my soul. Am I wearing a baseball cap over a tight ponytail, baggy dance pants and a tight tank top? That's my "I'm-desperately-writing-before-the-drop-dead-line" outfit and you can bet there's an editor breathing down my neck on the other end of the phone. Or am I wearing a sexy little satin slip over my naked flesh with a pair of candy-apple red open-toed high-heel mules revealing freshly painted toes? You can be assured that I'm writing something steamy and sexy, because that's my "Siren/Poetess" that needs to wallow in sensuality for the words to flow as silken as the slip.

The chains of the sling clang to the fierce rhythm of furious fucking. My trick-du-jour kisses me deeply and my legs fly and wrap around her. The 6" stiletto heel flies off my right foot and sails through the air. With reflex sharper then a cat's, she snatches the fetish slipper mid-air. Holding my small foot delicately, she places the slipper on it tenderly with the kiss of a prince. I swoon to a new level of arousal in the rightness of fucking in the perfect pair of shoes.

As you can see, my clothing items and I have a very intimate relationship. They speak for me. They arouse me. They are my vocabulary and aesthetic tools of self-expression. They are part of my seduction of myself and my courtship with others. Let's not forget that after all, I am a fetishist. Individual items arouse my libido. But it's not simply that a good pair of high heels or a tight pair of leather gloves will get me wet. There's a whole world and language of pleasure surrounding fashion for me. I suspect many other fetishists and sensual hedonists share the same experience.

First there is the pleasure of acquiring the heart throbbing garment of my desire. The process of acquisition can have the qualities of ritual or of treasure hunting. Seeking out the best pair of Wolford's stockings, requires me to make a pilgrimage to a city with the specialty shop, where I can find just the right pair, admire the packaging. Then I must have the discipline to stifle the thrilling desire to rip it open and slide it on right there. I travel home knowing that in the very bag next to me is the secret to pleasures and transformation.

The acquiring of bespoke clothing or custom-made garments has a particular and unique thrill for we garment-fetishists. I find the perfect craftsperson to make my garment, whether it's latex from Gaelyn & Cianfaran, Polymorphe or Vex, corsets from Puimond, customized dress shirts from Armani or leather dresses from Northbound or Madam S Leather. I take pleasure in finding places that create quality goods, with passion for the craft and excellent customer service. I will go to a place where I am understood, pampered and catered to. Having a bespoke garment made isn't simply about getting a good fit. It's about the process of making my fantasy a wearable reality. I want my aesthetic vision validated and then fleshed out. I want my shopping experience to be part of the excitement and anticipation building towards the erotic fulfillment of finally wearing the garment. I take pleasure in bringing in my sketches of outfits and ideas to the designer, then sitting down and working out the practical details, and then coming into the process of fittings. I become a significant part in the creation of my own visual and physical fetish drama. This is a very satisfying experience. Off the rack clothing, especially mass-produced and widely available items simply don't have this level of personal involvement and satisfaction. Fetish is a very personal pleasure. My garments should also represent such personal pleasure, history and involvement.

Sometimes a garment is acquired in a way that imbues it with personal history... I treasure the sapphire blue corset given to me by a beloved submissive. I think of her whenever I wear it. I feel the tightness on my waist as I would her arms wrapped around me in adoration. Each dinner out, each opera attended wearing that corset is a small outing with her. There's a pair of fetish heels that I bought with a lover while he was in contract to me as my submissive. I remember the swoon that came over him as he slipped them on my foot in the store. I remember how I laid my foot on his swelling sex through his jeans. I remember the sly kiss on the shoes right there in the store. Those particular shoes will never be worn for anyone else. Each garment bears witness to my passions, pleasures and history of decadence. They are my companions and consorts in pleasure.

Once a garment is acquired, then there is the pleasure of dressing! There are erotic choices for me here too. Shall I wallow in the pleasure of dressing myself? Shall I make a submissive dress me? Or will I take pleasure in being dressed by an adoring lover?

Dressing myself is an autoerotic pleasure. If I dress in solitude, the pleasure is profoundly narcissistic and inwardly directed. The focus is sensual and tactile. Sliding the tight leather gloves on, I become aware of my own body, with life coursing through every inch of it, and my hands throb as they are encased in the snug fitting black hide. In a fine pair of leather boots I admire the turn of my ankle. I caress the form of my body made into my own vision, confined, accentuated and protected in the corset. I may fantasize about the kiss on the boot from the submissive or the stroke from a lover's hand later that evening. But even in that, the central figure is me – the self and my body and senses. The process of self-adornment is also a process of self-expression and a fleeting act of artistry. Mood, thoughts, event type, purpose and creative intensity are all reflected in what I choose to wear and how exactly I will put it on. Will I simply throw on the platform clogs or will I take focus and attention to lacing up the boots. Do I feel contemplative or saucy?

Being dressed by my submissive is an imperious pleasure. I am the Queen at that very moment as the servant kneels before me to lace up my crotch high boots. The movies "Elizabeth" and "Star Wars: Episode 1 The Phantom Menace" both had exquisite scenes where the Queen is dressed and attended to by devoted servants. This is such a strong fantasy of mine from my childhood, that to this day, it moves me. It's not surprising that my servants and subs are taught how the finer points of distinctions between lingerie items, fabrics and pieces of clothing as well as how to care for them. In that moment, they are there to serve my pleasure and beauty.

On the other hand, being dressed by a lover is a different pleasure, where the locus of the attention is the equally shared relationship and the mutual pleasure. I also consent to be objectified differently than by the servant. My power is shifted from the Dominant Queen to the wanton siren of pleasures-to-come. The lover opens the new stockings with anticipation, unfurling them and admiring their delicateness. I watch her hands caress the stocking and long for her touch. With each item she decorates my flesh for our pleasure. With each item, she hides me from her sight, just for the moment, and increases the erotic tension for both of us. I become blazingly aware of her gaze. Her awareness of my beauty heightened, her touch becomes both feverish and reverential. Each garment promises potential for pleasure and adventures.

The fetish garment visualized, created and acquired now slides onto my flesh, oh so carefully... Now what? Sometimes that's simply all that's needed for me. At other times, however, I face the world and enjoy the pleasures of my fetish brazenly in the open, in full and grand view of the public. I wear it out! Sometimes I wear it out overtly, as I often do with my long latex gowns to the San Francisco Opera or a fancy dinner. At other times, however, it's a sweet little secret shared only with my self or my special companions.

When I wear my fetish garb secretly from the world, there's a different charge to the experience. I may be wearing a simple long skirt and blouse, but underneath I may have on a pair of long leather boots or a tight corset. I enjoy being secretly aroused under the guise of polite civility.

So, should you see me with a certain glow and satisfied smile that I carry through the day, perhaps now know why!

Those Fetish Wearin' Freaks

"Fetish Wear Strictly Enforced" reads the flyer in your hot kinky hands.

It's late spring; the leather social high season is upon us and the good perv's mind turns to the ever-important question: "What shall I wear?" Fetish wear, of course! The invitation guidelines for the various fetish and SM events often require you to arrive in appropriate fetish attire.

What's "appropriate fetish attire" anyway? Every one knows what that is, you say. It's kinky clothing, of course, you say. It's about sex, you say. You know it when you see it, you say.

Or do we? If I showed up at a fetish dress-code-enforced party in a latex jacket, rubber skirt, rubber gloves and high-heeled latex boots, their demon door guard would certainly let me in. If I showed up in a leather jacket, leather pants, leather gloves and leather high-heeled boots, the door demon will let me in. If I wore an Armani suit with Channel gloves and Blanik stilettos, the door demon would bark me away. Interestingly these are all variations on the same ensemble, yet, one is not acceptable, even if it arouses me sexually and creates a surge of power within to do some amazing D/s scenes. But what if I went off the deep end on my sexual scale? If I showed up in a full bunny suit, then you gotta' wonder what he'd do. He'd probably die laughing. If he keeled over off his stool and cracked his skull on the pavement, does that mean I get in?

The problem with assuming that we all 'just know' what fetish wear is, is much like saying that we know pornography from art when we see it. Your art may be my porn. (If you've ever watched me walk though the exhibitions at the Fashion Institute of Technology, you'll know what I mean. I get moist just thinking about it.) We often think that fetish wear is easily definable, yet the concept of fetish wear is so subjective and context dependant, it simply defies easy categorization. As much as we'd like to be able to do so.

Let's look at why people wear fetish clothing. After all a garment in itself is not an erotic entity. As an example, let's consider one of the 'staples' for fetish wear – leather boots. (Ok, I know some of you have begun to drool already….) Leather boots do not have sex on their own. Last time I looked in my closet there were no little leather loafers spawned by my thigh-high boots. Nor do they actively seduce people. (It's not the guns, it's the people. It's not the boots, it's the people.) Not all people who wear leather boots think they're having a sexual experience nor do they necessarily think that they're signaling for certain sexual behavior preferences. If they were, well, then all of the US Army would be one big sex orgy. After all, everyone there wears leather boots most of the time. What's relevant is the meaning that the person wearing the leather boots or looking at them attributes to those the leather boots… For that matter the meaning that a person attributes to any garment, is what makes that garment or material potentially a fetish clothing item.

Let's take a look at some of the different types of folks who wear fetish clothing…. These are but a few examples, and many people fall into multiple types depending on the occasion.

The Sexual Fetishists: Fetish wear for some people is strictly clothing that causes intense sexual arousal. It's not about fashion, dress codes or trends for them. It could be anything - leather corsets, boots, rubber diaper covers, Keds sneakers, even artificial limbs. The variations of objects that the person is attached to are potentially infinite because the creativity of the erotic human mind is potentially infinite. They may like to wear the item or have another person wear it. Some just like to handle the item. They may be happy at home with their fetish wear or might want to wear it out, sometimes showing, sometimes not. I'm a glove fetishist. It's very very erotic for me to wear leather gloves. I get off on it, whether someone is there or not, whether I'm out and about or not… This is what I'm feeling when I put gloves on…

164

The Romantic Fetishist: They find the object worshipped is a symbolic manifestation of the underlying power dynamics of their union with a given person. They may not find the object itself erotic, in the absence of a relationship to associate it to. They tend to be more relationally focused and are perhaps interested somewhat in sexual dominance and submission.

The Community Uniformists: They wear accepted or prescribed fetish garments almost as uniforms of their community of affiliation. It's not so much about personal sexual arousal as a sense of belonging and wearing items that indicate tribal identity. Sometimes it also shows their place in the historical continuity of their given community. The more traditional leathermen in the States often echo the romantic ideals ascribed to the 'old guard' leather men, who's images, in tern, came from post World War II military men and motorcycle club members. Many men and women today wear patches or pins from their leather clubs and events on their leather jackets or vests. This is not about eroticizing the pins and patches, but finding a common identity in kink and wearing the attire as community insignia. This is why some outsiders may get the impression that members of certain kink communities seem to be clones of one another. Other perv subcultures wear fetish clothing as a sort of a group uniform as well to reflect their community, although in ways that are perhaps less well documented then the American leathermen. For example, the Goth community also wears their attire as a form of community uniform with its own romantic ideals, aesthetics and sense of tradition.

The Artistic Expressives: These folks are literally a work of art on two legs. They find fetish-dressing events to be the perfect place to express themselves creatively and artistically. Body and fashion becomes the canvas upon which they create a moving expression of self, ideals, politics, humor, irony, dreams, beauty, and conflict. These and other messages are codified and represented in their garb. They do not see the clothing as a uniform for belonging, except in terms of satire and irony, as that would be limiting and express conformity to them. They may or may not eroticize their garments, but that's not the main concern for them at the moment. The exuberant self-expression of creativity is the central focus.

The Hipsters and Cultural Tourists: They wear fetish wear because it's trendy. They feel a vague sense of transgression in wearing "edgy" clothing and they wish to convey a sense of taboo-breaking, but since there is no community bond, historical context or personal sexual investment, the meaning of the items is stripped down to a vague notion of social transgression often fed by the media. Translation: they feel that they're cool and naughty but they don't really know why, except that they saw it on a music video. (I know, I sound a bit harsh. Yes, my perspective is biased, as I most often dress from some combination of the previously mentioned four types.) To their credit, some people in this grouping may be in a process of genuine self-discovery. They are sampling the range of potential cultures that they might fit into. They may be in search of something that's sexually fetishistic, or a community that they can belong to, but they haven't quite found the right thing yet.

The Respectful Outsiders: These are people who politely wish to honor the host's desire to create a space with a certain mood. As a kinkster, I really do appreciate the civility and respect of these folks. For a limited time of an evening's event, they wish be part of an underground community. Dressing in appropriate attire to go to a club might be the easiest way to get a taste of subculture tourism, make some interesting friends without any negative judgment from other folks or major life style changes. They make no pretense about the garment making them into something that they're not.

The Ticket In / The Bait: Some may also wear the fetish wear as a ticket into a cool nightclub or sex space. Some put on the fetish wear because it's seen as a way to attract sexually interesting potential partner but are not personally interested in the fetish items nor find them sexually arousing. You can spot them from a mile away. They're wearing the corset upside down and backwards. They might be the guy in leather pants (packaging crease still present) hitting on every woman wearing fetish-type clothing, thinking that wearing the garment alone indicates the woman's sexual availability to him. (Am I just a bit too obvious in my contempt of these folks?)

These are just some of the folks you'll see at the next fetish dress-code-enforced event you'll be at. Take a look around and see if you can recognize them! See you at the parties!

Getting Lucky at Fetish Parties

A beautiful woman teeters by on 10 inch spiked platform boots, clad from head to toe in a brilliant red latex cat suit, face hidden behind a mirror-eyed full hood with bright blue ponytails. Trailing behind her, on a chain leash and high stepping in black cloven-hoofed boots, is a half naked and muscular man cinched in a red leather corset, and a horse head hood. She cheerfully greets a 7' tall drag queen dressed in a PVC nun's habit and kisses the nun's girlfriend, dressed as a military officer with medals, riding boots and a bulging codpiece. Sweating and undulating bodies, clad in rubber and leather, pack the dance floor, gyrating to the DJ's spin magic. It's just another night in the fetish scene... and wouldn't you like to be a part of it?

The kink event high season is generally late spring to late fall, culminating around Folsom Street Fair (San Francisco) and the Skin Two Rubber Ball (London).

If you've never been to a fetish-theme party, you're really missing out on experiencing one of the flavors of major cities such as London, San Francisco, Toronto, New York, Amsterdam, and Berlin. Maybe you've wanted to go but you're not sure how to make the best of it? Or maybe you find yourself traveling around the globe to pervy hotspots and want to attend a fetish party, but you don't know where to get info. Let me, your very own Fetish Diva, help you get the most of your fetish party experience!

What are fetish parties like? Is there lots of sex and action?

First, you need to know that there are different types of fetish parties. The types of parties and focus of activities will vary by the local kink community standards, local laws, the general attitude around sexuality in the area, the organizers' goals and the availability of appropriate space. Some folks may imagine that fetish parties are non-stop sexual orgies in fetish wear. It's a nice fantasy, but usually it's not the case. Mind you, many fetish events are very sexy in mood, even when sex itself may be limited. Some parties function more like regular nightclubs with a fetish dress theme for added variety on the same old music. Some parties are gathering places for people who love bizarre costumes to congregate, see and be seen. It's a good place to meet like-minded fetishists for a future date or simply feel the warm glow of admiration and kinky glamour.

Each event varies in the degree of nudity and sexual contact allowed. Most fetish events I've been to seem to offer some sort of a formal SM play area. The quality and safety of the equipment available and the competence of the monitoring varies widely. If the place has a dungeon area, most likely bondage and basic spanking and floggings are acceptable. But this may very from State to State in the US and country to country beyond. Genital exposure, genital contact, oral sex or full-fledged intercourse, piercing or fire scenes are limited to different levels in each city. I remember going to a fetish party in Denmark. It was wild. They had the usual dance floor and play area, but people were having various sex all over the place. They even had the only heterosexually oriented "Black Room" I've ever been to. A "Black Room" is a totally dark room where people cram in together, hump, grind, fondle and get it on anonymously. I've generally known Black Rooms to be a feature of gay male parties.

It's important that you figure out what's considered acceptable behavior at each party and not expect more than that of the people you meet there. Otherwise you can get slapped by your object of desire, kicked out by burly, unforgiving bouncers, or worse, barred from ever coming back. Most events will try to describe what's expected. If expectations aren't spelled out clearly, then I suggest you go with the minimal expectations of simply seeing people in cool outfits, but be prepared for any action. Take a small toy bag or trick kit with your safer sex supplies, just in case. If you can't use it at the party, you might be able to use it back home with the cool new person you met there.

Do I have to wear fetish wear?

In one word: YES. If you want to have a good time, meet fun people and make the best of a fetish party, yes, you must wear some form of fetish wear that's appropriate for the event. Of course, you can choose not to wear fetish wear, but you might end up not being allowed into the party. If you get in the party with regular clothes on, by the sheer generosity or apathy of the door person, the attendees might ignore you or dis you as a simple gawker. Your chances of getting any action, even dancing with that cutie, will be like Frosty's chance in Hades. Some events will specify on their PR that they're encouraging or enforcing a certain look or theme, such as military uniforms, school uniforms, etc. Others will say that its "fetish wear required" or give a discounted entry for fetish wear, but not specify what's considered fetish wear. Generally they mean clothing made of latex, leather, PVC, uniforms, corsets and the like. In many places a black T-shirt and regular leather pants do not count as fetish wear. Find out before you go out. This is true for the guys as well as the gals. Dress codes are usually not gender biased. Speaking strictly for myself, I know that I would be far more interested in chatting with a guy or gal who takes the time to dress for an event in something really interesting. If you aren't wearing kink wear I might mistake you for facility staff, security, or the valet parking guy and not see you as one of the revelers.

This doesn't mean that you have to go out and spend a fortune on some exotic outfit. Fetish wear for a club can be done on a budget, although it'll require some creativity. PVC is the cheapest fetish wear and it's readily available. Even mall shops like Hot Topic and Frederick's of Hollywood sell PVC fetish type clothing. Military surplus stores and charity shops such as Salvation Army and Good Will are wonderful places to pick up old uniforms and transform them into wild and sexy fetish wear. If you want to go ultra budget, take a shiny black trash bag and electrical tape, make a T-shirt, skirt or pants out of it, hot glue tubes and computer chip boards onto it, paint your face like a science fiction character and bundle your hair in cables. Voila! You've got fabulously creative and futuristic fetish regalia for under $30.

169

Where do I find out about the next party?

One of the best ways to get info on what's happening in town is to find the best local fetish shop or sex-positive boutique, drop in and look for event flyers. While you're there, ask the shopkeeper about the events. Find out about the mood of each event, types of activities that happen there, dress code, etc. Checking out local free entertainment publications may help too. It's a bit harder to find a comprehensive on-line resource for each city, but they are out there. You might want to stop by my little yahoo discussion bulletin board and ask the other members there what's happening in a particular area. As they are from all over North America and Europe, they can give you some great suggestions. I often turn to the list myself for suggestions. It's a free board for the 18+ crowd at http://groups.yahoo.com/group/divamidori/

Now, go out and have a great time!

[You Asked!] What to Wear: Tips for Masculine Fetish Party Wear

Q. Dear Midori,

Since last year's Skin Two Rubber Ball, where we had a wonderful time... And now it's time to start thinking about the next Fetish Ball. And here's my dilemma. I've spent countless hours surfing the web to get a sampling of what the fetish world has to offer. And all of it is great. But why is that the fashion choices for men seem so limited? In comparison to women, what we men have to wear is downright plain. Now I'm no fashion hound or trendsetter, but when going to a fetish event it seems like the perfect time to make a statement. At the first event I wore black leather pants with a red zip-up latex vest. At another I wore black leather pants with a black leather vest and a black leather tieback head cover and accessorized with studded wristbands and a spiked collar. It's not that I'm envious of women in the fetish world, okay so I am, but I want to look like a man. I'm personally not into feminization or infantilism. Any suggestions? Naturally funds are not limitless. I would hate to go to the Ball again, bump into you and not look good.
MJ in LA

A. Hey Fetish-dude,
Oh, I feel for you. Ours is not the world of birds where the boys

170

are colorfully plumed and pretty and the gals are plain feathered. It is true that the easily accessible fetish shops seem to have little room for the creative man to express himself at a special event. We fetish-minded gals have it good for selections, I know. Fabulous cross-dressing is fun for many, but if it's not for you, then it's not for you. Today, some wise fetish wear retailers have come to recognize this niche. Consider uniforms, dear rubber-boy, uniforms! A sharp looking fantasy uniform is the solution to the butch fetish dilemma. Skin Two and House of Harlot, both excellent British latex makers have been making smashing and colorful rubber uniform for boys for years. An excellent corset maker, The Other Woman, is now making gentleman's uniform inspired waistcoat style corsets. For leather lovers, I know that North Bound Leather of Toronto and David Samuel Menkes in NYC are tops in making you look like a war hero in the trenches of fetish fashion. You might also consider the military look of the by-gone days. How about the medieval-butch look with chain mail? Put together a French Foreign Legion look from the local surplus store. Or take the cue from the movie "Gladiator" and don sandals or a leather battle kilt and a harness. (The last option is definitely the most comfortable in crowded party venues.)

Fetish & Erotic Photography

From time to time I find myself immersed in the world of photography. Here's some impressions from one such week in New York City a while back.

Shoot 1: The rigger binds the model's wrists, then runs the rope over the beam overhead. The model's arms jacked up behind, she twists her body to face the camera. The photographer emerges from behind the glaring lights to adjust her exposed breast over the tight corset.

Shoot 2: The art director refers to images of Western and Eastern deities to motivate the model's expression as the stylist adjusts her delicate veils. The photographer stopped clicking away to let the bondage rigger check for comfort and arrange the clothing.

Shoot 3: The location manager chatted with a resting model about Kant, philosophy, gender theory and art while another model draped herself over an Indonesian recliner and the photographer snapped happily away.

One of these shoots was for an adult/bondage web site. Another shoot was for capturing iconic images of fetishism. One was for an international mainstream high fashion magazine. So, which one was which? Can you guess?

No, dear readers, Shoot 1 was not for the porn site. It was for West East magazine, a very mainstream and hip magazine of haute couture fashion from Hong Kong. The model was from one of the best modeling agencies in New York, and casually chatted about globetrotting for Chanel, McQueen and Prada. A world recognized fashion photographer from Italy shot this at a highbrow commercial photo studio overlooking the Statue of Liberty. I had the pleasure of being the "Rope Artist" and "Rope Stylist" in collaboration with the photographer, creating a multi page fashion feature for a major European designer. The body positions were radical, sexual and provocative as were the items of clothing worn. The young model pouted her perfect lips to the camera and stretched out her long legs to emphasize the strain of the hard rope bondage. She stood on point in fetish ballet boots and stretched into near suspension. At no time, however, did we forget that this shoot was about fashion, beauty, fashion, art, fashion, sensuality and most of all selling fashion.

Shoot 2 was the adult/bondage web site photo shoot I art directed and rigged for a web site featuring my rope work. We didn't have a fancy studio or a budget bankrolled by a glossy magazine. We shot in hotel rooms and an auditorium after business hours. The models were professional bondage models, accustomed to sexually explicit shoots and "pink shots." They came having done their own well practiced "feature dancer" make-up of dark smoky eyes and bright red lipstick. They approached the shoot with athletic gusto and absence of any shyness around their exposed sex. Yet they also loved the creative reference to classical art. At no time, however, did we forget that this shoot was about creating erotic arousal for a commercial site.

Shoot 3 was a private project, an ongoing art photo collaboration between erotic photographer, Michele Serchuk and myself in creating images of sexuality that reflect our own libidos and emotional states. We shoot all over New York City, from dark alleyways to the rooftop of the Body Archive Museum in the Meatpacking District. (Back when it was still seedy.) She's shot my photo while I crawled through oil stained puddles, or covered in rubble, or in the sweltering heat and even in dampness just above freezing. This time we shot in luxury at a gorgeously appointed brownstone filled with fresh flowers. We focused on my fetishes... latex, high heels, satin slips, stockings, hot butches and leather gloves. Michele placed me in the dappled afternoon light and shot up the seductive line from my 5" stilettos and on up the seamed stockings. In the background Billie Holiday crooned as a muscular butch model, clad in well-packed leather pants, chatted about matters of philosophy and gender with our lovely host and location manager.

173

I just thought I'd share a little "behind the scenes" images of what it's like to be at photo shoots containing elements of fetish and bondage. I found it most ironic that the non-porn fashion shoot was far more demanding on the model than the bondage shoot.

This brings me to the topic of the role of the fetish photographer in shaping our experience of fetish and sexuality, both individually and culturally. On one of my jaunts back east I spoke in depth with Michele Serchuk, the New York based erotic photographer, over a long sultry night on this topic. My thoughts here reflect this conversation and thoughts that came from it. Her steamy images have graced the covers of erotic anthologies, magazines, "On Our Backs" magazine, exhibitions including a recent one at the Chrysler building and for MTV. She's also traveled to various cities to teach classes on how to bring out the Tigress in the Sex Kittens during personal erotic / boudoir photo shoots.

The erotic and fetish photographer serves many purposes when it comes to the documentation of eroticism. She is the chronicler of our sexuality as it stands at the moment for our culture as well as the individual. If parts of our culture finds stockings and garter-belts sexy, then these lingerie find their way in to her images. Vintage erotic photography gives us a glimpse into our cultural past on what we found erotic. These images also influence future generations of erotic image-makers. When I rope styled for Tiziano Magni, a regular photographer for Vogue, Marie Clair and Elle, He found inspiration in images shot by John Willie in the 40's. John Willie found his inspiration from images of 'damsels in distress' moving pictures and photos from Japanese bondage photographers. Nick Knight, top fashion photographer in the UK, who hired me as a rope stylist, drew inspiration from contemporary Japanese photographer, Araki, who's images are very sexual in their own right. Erotic photography and photography incorporating sexuality feeds on the libido of the world around them. In turn, the photographers feed and shape the future of sexually expressive art. When Fritz Lang showed the world the imperious, feminized and erotic robot in "Metropolis" he may have drawn from the classical Greek "Pygmalion" but he is still influencing images of the eroticized androids including photos by Helmut Newton, cyberpunk and landmark films such as "Blade Runner."

Beyond the role of cultural documentarian and shaper of sexual iconography, the erotic photographer is also on her own mission to express her own sexuality, which is 'of course a product of the greater culture within which she lives. Michele Serchuk became an erotic photographer in great part due to her frustrations with not finding sexual images reflecting her way of sensuality. As a woman who enjoys porn images of many types she would turn to magazines to whet her appetite and erotic imagination. Not finding images of sex and sensuality that represented her or what she wished to see, she grew increasingly disappointed and finally angry. Nothing portrayed her for who she was in her early 30's, 5'4" and 125lbs. Without images that reflected her in smut, she was, in essence, an invisible entity to the world, negated and erased in the eyes of society. Not one to settle for accepting the status quo, she turned her photographic eyes and skills to creating her own images of arousal. It was obviously a success, as proven by her photographic success record. With her very personal act of creating images to suit her turn-on, she also brings into focus and cultural existence a whole segment of sexual women. The erotic photographer serves to validate the existence individual in the eyes of society.

The erotic photographer also has a profound effect on the person being photographed. Michele Serchuk finds that women are consistently pleasantly surprised by the images from their photo shoots. Even the most sensually aware individual will not have a sense of his or her own beauty from another's gaze. The invisible eyes of the photographer can substitute for the gaze of the lover and that of society. Conversely it can also act as the critical and misogynistic gaze of the harsh world, but that's a whole separate discussion. When acting as the desiring and approving eyes of the lover, the photos created gives the 'model' a new visual language and self-awareness as a sensual being. Not only is she validated, but she may also discover her own visual sensual appeal that she was not previously aware of. A successful erotic photo shoot can positively change and amp up the sexual energy of the individual photographed.

Let's celebrate and enjoy the art created by the sexual, fetish and erotic photographers… or perhaps to make some of our own.

Confessions of a Fetishist

Let me climb atop my pedestal of power. I will stand on a pair of six-inch slivers of cold silver, like pristine icicle pillars upon which sits the castle of the Ice Queen. . Sliding my foot into the delicate opening I felt the warm silk caress of white kid leather lining. Power surges from the root of my ego through the perfectly hyper-extended arch of my delicate foot into my sex and shoots up to the base of my brain. The laces tighten the embrace of the leather onto my well-turned ankle. The second skin-hide covers my supple muscled calf. Gleaming hooks and eyelets shine cold and armor-like against all the slings and arrows that the world may hurl at me. I balance precariously with the well-practiced grace of the bound foot courtesan and stride forth with the determination of a warrior. The extreme pitch of the boot shank thrusts me forward into the world, to face life full on. No wallflower reticence for me.

Then the gloves.... Ahhh, the gloves. I part the opening ever so delicately, as if parting the petals of a flower... or the lips of my lover. They open for me and reveal the delights inside. My delicate fingers pressed together, I slide in. My eyes shut and my lips slacken as I take deep pleasure in my hands caressing the gentlest suede of unlined vintage kidskin gloves. My fingers unfold as the glove fingers surround me one digit at a time. As I reach the tightest portion, there's a slight resistance... then with the patient slow persistence of an experienced lover I push carefully forward... spreading and warming, but never forcing and never tearing... eventually the leather gives way to me and lets me in fully. I stretch my fingers in their tight encasement. They are so tight that I can feel my hands throb in them. I can feel my own heart beat. I am aware of my sensual existence. My hands raised before me, I close my eyes and wallow in the slow throbbing, the gradual quickening and the seeming swelling throbbing of my hands.

My head reels in a state of full fetish pleasure. Dressing is the process of self-seduction... foreplay between me and myself, between the person in the mirror and the objects of her desire.

I have many lovers. Let me name a few... The drawer full of size 6 1/4 vintage leather gloves of all lengths. My tough yet supple leathers that transform me into a black skinned warrior angel. The red patent open toed mules that tantalize the world with the nakedness of my perfectly formed arch. The corset that embraces me so tightly that I'm breathless with desire. The latex with its intoxicating scent that transmits all touch into vibrating shivers. The primal comfort of furs that gently caresses me. The particular shade of red lipstick promising the potential for the perfect kiss... There are so many more.

Sex is an expression of aesthetic passion for me. I am profoundly turned on by things that are intensely aesthetically beautiful and sensual. My sexuality is not genitally focused, but rather it's diffuse, encompassing a range of objects, senses and areas of the body. I am a fetishist. Sex for me is about my senses being in a heightened state of arousal and the constant search for the artistically perfect moment of power and form.

As my fetishism is the state of arousal I find through taking pleasure in the beauty of form, my desire extends beyond clothing and objects to the body – my own, my lover's and my submissive's. I do not paint, but I dress in strokes of color and textures of expression. I have never studied ballet, but I will let my glances dance and choreograph the expressions of my butterfly hands.

I take pleasure in the lovers who stride in perfecting their physical form and those blessed from birth with gifts of beauty... A lean sculpted body... Spirit filled dreadlocks... A well-muscled back... There is a dancer I desire who creates a conflict of desires in my heart just by being who she is. Do I stand near her to take in the honeyed fig scent of her skin, or do I watch from across the room so I may see her full form in graceful and sinuous movement? There is a man I see at the gym whose grimace and pained focus are delicious. There's a queen whose attention to detail in transformation is utterly mesmerizing.

In my SM scenes, aesthetic perfection makes me delirious. My bondage is constantly in search of that balance of architectural, organic and sexual beauty. I need a flogging to become the kinetic art of two people's desire. When I transform a man into a woman or a woman into a man, I must at the end be able to fall in love with my creation... Let Galatea live again. I, Pygmalion, am constantly creating, searching, envisioning.

The fetish object is a symbolic manifestation filled with the promise, a potential for fulfillment and the moment of perfection. The fetishist is thus in a perpetual search for that elusive moment of blissful fulfillment, a joining with perfection. Since the kind of perfection that is so exactingly sought is, by definition, impossible, the fetishist is forever on this quest, a doomed journey in search of ultimate sensual bliss. The fetishist, however, unlike the protagonist of the Flying Dutchman actually does not seek release from this perpetual search, but revels in the constant tension created by the never fulfilled hunger.

By nature or by choice I have imbued objects with the power to arouse me. I know that I am on this quest for the unattainable moment. Yet I am happy with this constant state of dreaming. It's delicious, being forever slightly hungry.

As a fetishist, I am inherently a voyeur and an exhibitionist simultaneously. I swoon over the sight of a perfectly dressed Leatherman, who in turn finds arousal and appreciation beyond his orientation in the artistic creation that is me. In my public play scenes I delight in the creation of erotic motion before others and simultaneously find pleasure in watching the beauty of my play partner's powerful movements.

When my mind wonders, where do I find entertainment? What's a fetishist's pornography? My porn magazines are Elle, Vogue, W and Shuz.. Mainstream fashion magazines are filled with powerful fetishistic images. The book *Shoes: A Celebration of Pumps, Sandals, Slippers & More* is never far from my fingertips at my office. At any time I can flip through its well-worn pages to find my pulse quicken at the sight of a divinely crafted pump or boot.

Yes, my sexuality is decidedly not genitally based. At times I even find genitally obsessed sexuality to be somehow grotesque. I

178

realize that the argument could be made that genitally-focused eroticism is only natural as it's directly reproductive and makes sense from the perspective of sexual drive for the sake of propagating the species. Some may say that my removal of erotic response from reproductive concerns is indicative of unhealthy modern sexuality. On the other hand, the re-wiring of erotic desire and the hyper-connection of symbolic entities with my sexual response may also be the natural extension of extremely well developed and complex gray matter that's capable of making strong new symbolic associations. Fetishism may indeed be an expression of the complex evolution of the human brain.

As a fetishist I am totally devoted to sensual pleasure, even if that comes at the cost of denying immediate and basic sexual gratification. A mere orgasm is nothing to me compared to an object possessing in itself the potential for perfection of beauty and power and possessing also the capability of transmitting to me the potential for greater beauty and power...

Forget the Hitachi Magic Wand. Give me the Blahniks!

Part Four: Tips & Tricks for Adventurous Sex

Photo by Steve Diet Goedde

IN THIS CHAPTER...

Time to sample some fun kinky sex tips!

Over the years I've written several sex advice columns and provided erotic tips for various magazines and publications. They range from the mild to the wild. For this chapter I picked some of the pervier ones for our entertainment. Think of this chapter as an assorted sampler box of delectable erotic techniques. If you like what you sample here there are books, classes and other resources out there with more in depth information. I chose to retain the Q & A format and have made only slight changes to the text. I thought it would be fun this way and figured that the people who submitted the questions originally just might enjoy seeing them in print! Since I wrote these for magazines such as On Our Backs and Taboo, most frequently I will be writing about playing with female bottoms, so the pronoun will be she. But when it comes to most types of play, such as nipple play, wax play, flogging, etc, the gender or genitals are not too relevant. So if your intended love-target is a guy, just mentally adjust my "Her" to your "Him." The tone is pretty cheeky and smutty, but that's what you get when you write for sexy and smutty magazines!

How to Get into SM Online & Finding Partners

Dear Midori,

> *I want to get into S&M but I don't have anyone to do it with. I've met some people who seem to be good candidates to get started with. I figure finding an S&M partner and doing it on the Net would be the safest and best way to get going. Any advice?*

Hopeful in Springfield

Dear Hopeful

Why waste your time on faux play when you can get the real and juicy stuff? The Internet is fine for getting good info on safer play, and for finding out where the cool events and local clubs are. It may also be a good place to find a person to play with in the flesh. But the Net as the primary resource SM play sucks for getting you any quality experiences, building long lasting SM relationships or getting you some really hot action other than the one-handed variety. It's great for fantasy play, but it ends there. Sure, it's safe, but so is phone sex. It's not like you can spank your network and stick your dick in the disk drive slot. If you're willing to find folks on line to turn it into a face-to-face relationship then you have some real potential for getting your rocks off in a serious way. Beware the players who only want to interact on-line. They're not looking to explore a SM relationship. They're looking for adult fantasy role-playing... Remember the phrase "Buyer Beware." The hot twenty-three year old D cup slave girl you're chatting with might be the hairy 53-year-old guy in the cubicle next to you. The experienced old-guard mistress might be some pimply-faced frat boy. When the computer turns off, so does the relationship. There's no aftercare once the digital connection is dropped. In general you'll have a better time finding a relationship in the real world where you can explore and grow, make friends that'll give you sound advice and actually whip, get whipped, fuck or get fucked.

Nothing replaced the caress of actual hands on excited flesh. There's no on-line substitute for actual leather or latex on a wet cunt. No Internet play can replace the emotional and physical impact of a righteous over-the-knee spanking.

So use the Net to find the hottie of your dreams and meet them in the flesh. For a thorough listing of BDSM clubs and organizations in each state and major cities in the USA see http://www.darkheart.com/sceneusa.html. For a good site to meet BDSM play partners of just about every taste, proclivity and perversion every where check out http://www.bondage.com

Advice for the Traveling Kinkster

Dear Midori,
I'm leaving for LA soon with a carry-on suitcase half full of toys... I was wondering, since you travel a lot you might be able to give me any advice on what to say to the x-ray people if they say anything.

Thank you,
Toy-Princess, San Francisco

Dear Toy-Princess,

I've had a few incidences with security folks in the course of my globetrotting.

The best thing to do is to pack all your toys into the checked luggage. If you have any doubt at all about your toys, check it. Make sure that your luggage is securely shut, where nothing will drop out and no one can slip things out of it. I prefer a hard shell suitcase so it won't rip in its transit; that also keeps my canes and other toys from getting mangled. Lately the security policies won't allow bags to be locked. Count on the fact that your bags will be rifled through, whether checked or carry-on. If you have small things, such as clothespins, make sure to pack them in see-through bags. Plastic freezer bags or even clear jewelry bags designed for travel are fantastic.

Note that many common SM toys are considered high security risks and weapons by the legal authorities. Never, ever pack police style or metal handcuffs, blades, pocketknives, nun-chukus, sjambock, stun guns, or weird electronic toys in your carry-on. At minimum, they might be confiscated and you'll never see them again. At worst, you'll be detained, arrested, charged and go to court, plus lose all your stuff and miss your flight. My friend Molly had her bag torn apart by Heathrow security looking for what they thought was a bomb. They found her set of hot rollers. Innocuous things like metal lipstick tubes may look like explosives to them as well.

I remember in Burbank where I had a Sarah Lashes whip in my carry-on. It has a steel core in the handle so it showed up in the x-ray, and sure enough they wanted to see it. The gray-matter-challenged security guy pulled out my whip and started swinging it around this way and that as everyone in the line waited and stared. Laughing, he asked me what it was for. I smiled a placid smile and loudly told him, "It's for kinky sex. I'm sorry if it's still sticky." (Of course the flogger wasn't sticky. I always thoroughly clean my toys.) He turned bright red, shoved the flogger back into my case and let me catch my plane.

I have found that smaller airports in the US have really incompetent security and larger American airports often have needlessly power hungry security. These are both annoying. European airport security tends to be professional and calm but they won't let you get by if they feel any suspicion toward you at all.

So, pack wisely, and if they ask, tell them rather loudly that your items are sex toys for kinky sex. Be unmoved and say it with a straight face. It'll embarrass them more. It works! Of course, I might not try that in very religiously conservative countries… Caveat emptor.

Happy travels!

Nipple Play: Clamps and Suction Cups

Dear Midori,

Tell me about nipple clamps. What are the good types and bad ones? How long do I leave them on? How come people like them? How do I make my girlfriend like them?

Clamp-curious in Chicago

Dear Clamp,

Nipple clamps are the greatest things to get those little pink pearls to pay attention to your ministrations. If used right, they'll help her ride the crest of pleasure and pain… they can even be an orgasm trigger for some babes. The more you play with these two little buttons, the more responsive and more easily turned on they'll be. But if you do that incorrectly, it'll just annoy the hell out of her.

There's actually no way to "make" your girlfriend like nipple clamps… or anything, for that matter. The secret here, my clamp-happy friend, is to seduce her into enjoying nipple clamps… or whatever else you have in mind. Chicks love being seduced. You're not some teenager getting some quick back seat action here. Invest a little time. Not sure how she likes her breasts or nipples touched? Start slow and soft, all over them, circling down to her areolas and nipples. Does she like it? You've got the green light to go heavier. Increase the strength of your touch. Eventually go for light pinching, and then to heavier pinching. Try pinching the tip of the nipple, middle of the nipple to the base and to behind the nipple. This 'hands-on' research will help you figure out exactly what level of pressure to use and where she likes it.

Now that you have the basic research done, you need to go gather a sampling of all sorts of clamps to try out. (Who said homework's no fun?) You can gather a whole mess of different types for a song. For commercially produced nipple clamps you can always try kinky specialty stores or sex shops. There you can find assortment of ready to use models. These often come with a chain connecting them and rubberized tips. The chain is great to keep you from losing the clamps in the drawer like socks in the dryer. The chain also offers a hitch to tie the clamps off to a stationary object like your head board, the back of a chair, her bound toes or even to separate clamps attached to her labia! You can make her hold the chain in her mouth for that added lift that she's always wanted for her bodacious ta-tas. (Of course, if she drops the chain or if the clamps come off, you might have to dole out some fun discipline! How about some light weights to attach to the clamps?) The rubberized tip is really a nice touch. Many of these clamps have gnarly teeth that would break delicate skin, so the rubber-dipped tips protect her. They also help to keep the tips from sliding off. A dash of baking powder or cornstarch on her nipples and areolas will also prevent clamp slippage. Remember to use cornstarch or baking-POWDER, not baking soda. Baking soda is very abrasive to the skin in a non-sexy way.

There are some excellent basic ready-to-use clamps. The 'tweezer' style with two thin prongs and adjuster loops are very popular, even with lighter or newer players. Any of the adjustable models are a good buy. Many have little screws that modulate the bite of even the scariest looking clamps, making them as mean as alligators or as gentle as butterflies. These vicious looking but adjustable styles are wonderful if you want to have a bit of the psychological upper hand and keep her on her toes. It's a good thing. The 'clover' clamps are really pretty looking, but they can pack a punch. Originally made as Japanese embroiderer's clamps, they tighten when they're pulled on. These are good for moderate to heavy players, as they don't have an adjustable setting level for 'light.'

Go hunting for some creative clamps at hardware stores and office supply stores. Plain ol' wooden clothespins come bagged by the hundreds. Plastic and metal memo clips and file clips are fun! Small grip clamps used for model making look really sinister and yet are gently adjustable. If the teeth of any of these clamps are too sharp or ragged, consider filing them down or dip the business end in tool-dip.

Now put your pervert's research and scavenger hunting skills to work. Put clamps on the spot on her nips that you know she likes. As with any sort of play, start out lightly and gradually get more intense while gauging her turn-on. This suggestion applies to the intensity of the pressure as well as duration of clamping. At first leave them on for just a few minutes and take them off. Kiss and caress those tormented nipples. The gentle pressure and strain of the clamps on the nipples might feel good to her in a new way. Then there's the moment of clamp removal. The sensation of blood rushing back into the area when the clamps are removed might feel even more excruciatingly sweet and possibly more memorable. Each time leave the clamps on longer to figure out how long is right for your gal. At first most people are quite sensitive and can take only a little bit. With regular play, however, soon she'll be asking for more. Pass the first time successfully? Try clamping on multiple clamps on each breast at a time. Getting advanced? Flick the clamps and watch her shudder!

Let's talk positioning of the clamps. It's best to get some flesh and not just skin between the teeth of the clamps. Aim to place them just at the base of the nipples or even on the areola of the nipples. This produces a really hot engorgement of this erogenous zone. If you only pinch the skin at the tip of the nipples then you'll only cause an awfully distracting and non-sexy sensation that's hard to eroticize even for hardened masochists. Remember that it's not just about creating pure pain, it's about creating intense pleasure, so try to avoid creating random discomforts. You can always ask her if she can take more of the clamps in her service to you.

Of course you should also try it on yourself. Strictly for research, of course! This way you'll know better the sensation you'll be creating in her. It's a good idea to do this before just about anything you might want to try on your sweetie. For further advice, check out the book, *The Toybag Guide to Clips and Clamps* (Greenery Press) by Jack Rinella

Dear Midori,

How about a few words on using suction cups on tits? Where do I get them?

Tit Lover, Wisconsin

Dear Tit Lover,

Suction cups are another great way of getting your sugar-tit's perky attention. Many are designed as plastic cups that attach to a pump action handle that creates little pockets of suction. It pulls the entire nipple up, into the cup, engorging and swelling it temporarily. It works just like a miniature cock pump. Some of these cups are made so you can remove the pump handle away from them while still leaving the cup attached to the nipple. As soon as the vacuum on the cup is broken, however, the nips go back to their usual size – just like when you remove a cock pump.

I like to leave the cups on for a while and play with the breast. It feels really new and exciting to many women when the attached cups are jiggled, tapped or even buzzed with a vibrator. The suction action, like sucking on the nipples with the mouth, makes them more sensitive to other kinds of touch, even after the cups are removed. Once they're removed, try sucking, pinching, clamping or licking the nipples to see how charged and sensitive they are. Put the cups on and take them off several times for effect. Some women might even start to milk after a series of serious cupping sessions. Usually there isn't much cause for concern if a slight amount of fluid leaks form the nipple. If you and your sweetie are worried, she should consult her doctor.

You might have some problems with the vacuum suction needed to keep the cups from falling off. Wetting the rim of the cups really helps for this. I like to make the gal lick the cup well with her lusty wet tongue, demonstrating her oral talents for me. Make sure that there's no hair where you're trying to cup. That can break the seal too. This is a problem is you want to use the cup on someone's clit. Shaving or tweezing works for that, particularly around the cunt.

Yes, I said 'around the cunt.' Cupping the pussy is a nasty little trick I like to do. It works just like those penis pumps you see advertised. Except with a babe you aim for the clit, so you have to use a smaller cup or cylinder, or the same sort of cup you'd use for the nipples. Push the lips apart, pull up the clit hood, stick the spit-slicked cup around the clit and pump a stroke or two. Don't over pump her. The clit's so sensitive that more than a few strokes and it no longer feels good.

Soon, the clit will puff up and fill the cup while she's moaning and writhing in newfound surge of cunt sensation. With her swollen clit captured in the plastic cup, now she's under your sexual control. Again, tapping or jiggling the cup will make her squirm uncontrollably. Placing a vibrator against it will make her climb the walls with pleasure! Then, slide the cup off and finger her clit or go down on her and lap away at her tender morsel while you finger fuck her or do her with a dong and she'll literally melt into a giant puddle of orgasm in your hand.

You can get cupping devices and pumps at sex shops, or SM shops. You can order them from places like Mr. S Leather in San Francisco or on-line at the Stockroom. (http://stockroom.com) You can also find them in places where they sell Asian health care supplies. Try shops in your local China Town and look for something called a 'cupping set.'

Hot Wax Play

Dear Fetish Diva Midori,

I saw some S&M movies using candle wax. It looked great. I want to try it on my wife. Am I supposed to use special candles? Got any tips before I get started?

Hot & Bothered, California

Dear H&B,

You're talking about "Hot Wax" scenes. Playing with heat or cold can be really arousing because it gets the nerves and the body all pumped up and primed with endorphins. Ask your honey if she's up for it. Then, if she'd prefer, tie your baby up all sweet and sexy, drip some hot wax on her, tingle up her skin just right and next thing you know, she just might be writhing in pleasure and ready for a righteous fucking! (The bondage is optional. I just thought I'd throw it in there for fun!)

The choice of candles is most important. Don't just go and grab some old candle off the dining room table. The wrong candles can cause some pretty nasty burns on her skin. Then she'll be pissed off and you'll be in the doghouse for a while. Paraffin candles are cheap and melt at a lower temperature than beeswax candles, which is good (the cooler the melt, the safer the candle). Perfumed candles and candles with glitter in them seem to burn much hotter than the paraffin ones. Those tall candles in glass used for church altars are often made of paraffin and sold cheaply. You can get them in many shades, which will make your hot wax play more colorful. Make your own kinky Jackson Pollacks on your babe's bod. Make sure to test the temperature of the melted wax on your own skin before using it in kinky sex play.

Before you start dripping the wax, have her lie on old sheets, a drop cloth or old towels because this can get really messy. If she's not clean-shaven and slick skinned, rub her down well with baby oil. This keeps the wax from getting caught up in pussy hair and other body hair and ripping it out upon removal. Bad ouch!

I like to aim at the breasts, back, belly and limbs. I tend to avoid the face and head hair, although sometimes I'll drip wax onto a tongue stuck far out. Hot wax play on the tongue is really psychologically intense. Hot wax on the cunt is fun, but start with other parts first. Once you're prepped, hold the lit candle high above your target area. This way the wax is cooler when it hits her skin. Check to see that she's enjoying the sensation. Then you can lower it gradually, which increases the temperature of the wax on her skin.

Tired of little droplets and the time it takes to cover an area? Get a tiny crock-pot and metal ladle to dedicate just for wax play. Put some paraffin in it. You can get these at craft stores or beauty supply stores. Melt it to a nice temperature and just ladle it on. Again, be really careful with the temperature of the wax.

It's a good idea to have a bowl of cold water and a towel near by just in case. For more details on wax play and safety check out *The Toybag Guide to Hot Wax and Temperature Play* from Greenery Press.

Whipping & Flogging

Dear Midori,

My girlfriend wants me to whip her before I fuck her but neither of us know much about it. Are there different types of whips? What should I go for?

Doc, Idaho

Dear Doc,

You lucky devil! There are lots of different kinds of whips you can get depending on what effect you want. Don't pick up a whip just because it's cool looking. I suggest you start off sweet and soft and move up in intensity based on how much she's getting off on all of it. Some of the softest floggers will be made of buttery soft suede, rabbit fur, soft strands of fluffy nylon and other such materials. Other types of leather make harder whips. Some whips are made of still other materials such as rubber or even chain. While some whips might look really cool, they might not feel good at all on her skin. Check out what it feels like first on your self before flogging your honey. There are many whip makers out there you can choose from. Some of my favorites are The Toy Bag, Lashes by Sarah, Fred Norman and Happy Tails. Try shopping at places where there are many different types of floggers, whether a shop or a kinky vendor fair. The more types you try out the better. San Francisco's SM Community Exchange and Boston's Fetish Fair Fleamarket are both semi annual SM vendor fairs. In Chicago don't miss the massive vendor area during the International Mr. Leather weekend.

It's easier to aim accurately with shorter-tailed whips, while it's much harder to control long tails when you first start off. Shorter tailed whips are also good to use while fucking as you can keep close to her. The diameter of the handle is also important. If it's too thin or too thick you'll waste energy gripping the whip, you'll get tired faster and your control will be compromised.

With any flogger meaner than a fluff ball, you'll want to be careful about where you're hitting. Avoid the kidney area, head and face. It's also not a good idea to strike on bony parts. Large muscled areas like the upper back and ass are great. Some women really get wet having their cunts whipped. Whacking her tits can be fun, but it's best to aim at the pectoral muscles above the tits. If she's had a boob job or cysts or is nursing a kid, make sure to check in with her to see if breast flogging feels good or not.

You'll learn lots about how to flog well by watching others do it. When possible take a hands-on workshop. Then practice on your own until you feel comfortable. You can also get fantastic info on whipping from Joseph Bean's book, *Flogging*.

Bullwhips

Dear Fetish Diva Midori,

Ever since I saw the image of a bound, aroused and helpless Catherine Denuve being whipped in the classic movie Belle du Jour *I've gotten off to the idea of using a bullwhip on a woman. Is this possible or should I just keep it in my jerk-off fantasies?*

Indiana Johnson, Miami

Dear Indiana,

Oh, that was a hot scene with Ms. Deneuve so ravishingly ravished! The image of the cruel dominant with a bullwhip is a classic SM image – a penultimate symbol of sadistic sexual power. These single shaft whips come in various different styles, often called single-tails, signal whips, snakes and bullwhips. The different names indicate different styles of whips.

Yes, people do use this on each other for hot SM sex and it can be really exciting. Used with skill these whips can softly caress and sensually tease a submissive into a frenzy of juicy arousal and provoke their desire to submit further. The snake can lash into the skin with hot precision delivering just the jolt that the masochist craves, leaving red welts that are sensitive to caresses for days.

The problem with single-tailed whips is that they're damned hard to control and to learn how to use safely. Not only can bad whip technique take an eye out, damage a major organ or permanently maim the bottom, but the top can also hurt herself! It's so embarrassing when you hurt yourself in front of the submissive! That makes having to visit your bottom at the hospital even worse.

Another problem with the single-tail whip is the cost. A quality whip can set you back two or three C-notes easy. If you actually want to hit a person with it, you need to get a quality tool. The cheap 'Halloween whips' can never be used with any accuracy and you're sure to make a fool of yourself. Of course if you just want a whip for the menacing visual effect, go for the dime-store bullwhips. There's nothing wrong with having it just for a prop.

If you want to actually use it on a person, start by using it really softly. Begin by using it like a silk scarf and caress her softly, slinking it around the body like a snake. Use it as an extension of your arms and wind it around her and pull her into you. Then, when you're alone, without anyone around, including your bottom, do like Harrison Ford did in preparation for Indiana Jones. Put on head protection with a safety goggles, a leather or denim jacket, long pants and gloves. Find an open space and practice with various techniques. Set up some targets and improve your control. You'll need to learn how to touch the target softly as well as to hit it with force. The control you have is the key. The video "Whip Cracking with the Masters Vol. I" by Anothony De Longis and Colin Dangaard of by The Australian Stock Saddle Company is a good visual guide, although it's not at all meant for the SM audience. *The Bullwhip Book* by Andrew Conway is a good book to learn how to swing the whip. If there's a circus arts school or rodeo arts school near you, you might want to take some classes on how to use stock whips and bull whips. I'll be honest with you, many instructors at such schools are not kink friendly, so you might not want to share your sexual reason for seeking their tuition.

Once you're ready to use it on your sex-slave babe, you might want to start with her fully clothed and protected. A leather hood will serve double duty to protect her head and face and put her in deeper submissive space. A towel on the neck, a leather or denim jacket and pants or even a bondage bag would be a good start.

What ever you do, practice, practice, and practice.

Spanking & Corporal Punishment

Dear Midori,

Tell me about spanking! My wife and I want to play with her being the naughty little girl.

Discipline Minded, NY

Dear Disciplinarian,

Oooh, now that's juicy! I can just see her in a cute little school uniform, bent over the end of a desk with white cotton panties pulled down just below the ass cheeks. You'd be standing over her, wearing the principal's suit and gazing down sternly over heavy rimmed glasses. You tell her that she's been a very naughty girl and that this correction is for her own good. She whimpers, shakes her head and sticks her ass out further, showing her dripping cunt in the most enticing way... You raise your hand and bring down your cupped hand to her soft ass cheeks making a loud slap. Your hands cup her warm ass and she moans and wiggles against your hand.

We're talking about classic corporal punishment! It can involve spanking, caning, paddling and rulers. The ass is the most common target, but her cunt, the palm of her hands, the soles of her feet or her inner thighs might be good too... depending on what her 'infraction' was. The turn on is about playing with power and the guilt of being turned on as a naughty kid being punished by an authority figure. . Costumes can make it really spicy. Schoolgirl and teacher outfits are, of course, hot. So are the make-believe games of daddy's little girl or mommy's naughty boy with the outfits to go with them. If you like Victorian scenes, you can play as the governess and her ward.

There's always some infraction on the part of the disobedient girl that needs to be corrected. Bending her over a bench or your own lap will really make her feel helpless and exposed. Make her admit or confess to her supposed misdeeds. It's spicier if these have to do with sexual mischief such as being caught masturbating or showing her pussy to another boy. Have her tell you in great detail. Then firmly announce that she needs to be corrected and do so solemnly. In the course of this, the fantasy schoolteacher might be tempted to take advantage of this helpless girl sexually.

Dear Midori,

I want to get a spanking from my boyfriend... maybe give it too! I just want to try it. So what do I need to know? How do I get him into it?

Bratty Princess, Houston

Dear B.P.

Have you asked him? I'd be willing to bet my spike-heeled boots that, if you naughtily mentioned that it would really turn you on even more if he gave you a sweet spanking on your willing behind, he'd jump to the opportunity! Maybe the two of you could agree to play a sort of Spanking Poker. It's like strip poker but for you it's about spankings!

A good warm-up is essential for an erotic spanking. Of course if the spanking is a punishment fantasy, you may not want a warm up and just go for the gusto. Otherwise, start with a soft caress on the fleshy part of the bottom; work up to light taps, and slowly up to heavier strikes. Varying the pace and intensity instead of a straight ramping up of intensity helps the body to eroticize the sensation and eventually get dripping wet or hard from it. Yes, you can get a sopping wet cunt or ragingly hard cock just from a sweet, slow spanking!

The position is pretty important. It's hardest on the body to support one's own weight, such as standing or holding one's own ankles. If you want the spanking to be an 'ordeal' to be endured, you may choose that route. On the other hand, if comfort is your goal, lying down on a soft surface like a bed or couch seems to be the easiest for the body. There are some really sexy positions too. Having a person over the knees feeds a lot of fantasy roles. Wedging a male submissive's cock between the dominant's thighs can be highly arousing, stimulating and even erotically embarrassing. Having the bottom bent over with their head trapped between the dominant's thighs can be a very powerful position. Of course you can reverse this so the dom is sitting on the sub's face as she grabs his legs and spanks away. Spanking during sex is fun too, although you may have to get a bit creative with your positions.

Make sure that you're hitting the fleshy full part of the butt, near the bottom of the cheeks. That's often called the 'sweet spot.' Avoid the kidneys, the tailbone and the sides of the hips. Strikes to these areas generally don't' feel as erotic, to varying degrees, and can cause nasty injuries. Spanking the pussy along with the cheeks can be a super hot experience for many women. Some guys like light taps on their balls with the spanking too. Of course if you have a butt plug shoved in your submissive's ass, a light spank can be shudderingly hot for them!

You can use your bare hands for a classic spanking. If you find your hands stinging more than the bottom's butt, then try wearing tight leather gloves. The sensation of leather will be sexy for the bottom too. Leather straps or belts can be fun, but make sure not to use the metal buckle or ornamental studs on the butt. Other creative instruments can include a good book (or 'the Good Book' for certain fantasies), the sole of a shoe, a birch cane, a frat paddle or more. For an old fashioned scene, try a wooden hairbrush.

Some resources:
* *The Complete Spanker* by Lady Green
* *Naughty Spanking Stories from A to Z* by Rachel Kramer Bussel
* *The Toybag Guide to Canes and Caning* by Janet Hardy

Enjoy!

Gags

Dear Midori,

Gags are so sexy! I've been turned on by images of captive gagged women in movies and comic books since I was a kid. The duct-taped mouth is especially hot. I've been wondering, though, some gags look really uncomfortable and I'm kind of worried about using one on my girlfriend. How will I know if she'll like it? Any suggestions?

Gag Boy, Seattle WA

Dear Gag Boy,

A luscious pair of red lips stretched helplessly around a demanding gag as her eyes plead for mercy and her moans beg me to take her even deeper... Just think of those classic Betty Page photos! Oh, yes, gags are big turn-on for lots of people.

Whether or not your girlfriend will like gags, I don't know. You'll have to ask her. If she doesn't know, try a small gentle gag with her consent and see what she thinks of it. If the gag is uncomfortable or causes injury, she won't find it a turn on, so here are a few things to consider in making your fantasy of gag play a juicy reality.

Many gags can seriously impede breathing. If she's congested, asthmatic or has other problems breathing a gag that seals off the mouth is a bad idea. Avoid the solid ball gag style and the rubber inflatable types, and certainly avoid taping the mouth shut. If she's experiencing limited breathing you can still play with gags as long as they still allow mouth breathing. A horse bit, a horizontal bar shaped gag or a strip of cloth or scarf that she can bite down onto, are great for this. Many bottoms love gags they can bite down on. This can fuel their fantasy of being the struggling captive or help them to process a painful sensation and turn it into pleasure. Make sure that any part of the gag that's in the mouth isn't made of metal or any other hard material that could chip the teeth. I'd hate to see how cross her dentist would be with you.

SM equipment makers such as Mr. S or the Stockroom make gags that force the mouth open such as O-rings, piss gags, surgical mouth spreaders or breather gags that combine a mouth stuffing sensation with a tubular shape for better breathing.

These gags that force the mouth open are not just safer for breathing, but are hotter for the increased vulnerability of the bottom and control by the dominant. With her wet mouth forced open, she knows she's helpless against anything that you might want to stuff into that gaping accessible hole.

Just because a gag is supposedly made for SM, by a toy manufacturer doesn't make that the right gag for your girlfriend. Big red ball gags are sexy looking on the shelf, but some manufacturers must never actually play with SM themselves, as many of the gags I see at cheap sex shops would barely fit into the mouth of a horny hippo much less a delicate-mouthed babe! When in doubt get the small sized gag. If the ball gag is too big, she's going to strain her face too much, split the sides of her lips or injure the TMJ (tempero-mandibular joint) and generally feel awful and not horny. You'd be better off taking a practice golf ball (looks like a smaller wiffle ball) and stringing a leather thong through it. This low-tech solution often makes the best gag for folks.

A few other pointers... When you tie the straps around the head, make sure that they're not too tight as that can also cause discomfort and injury. A really simple and effective, although slightly weird looking option is the sports mouth guard.

The duct-tape image from movies and SM illustrators like Bob Bishop really cranks up many of our libidos. Unfortunately it's not a practical option for many submissives. I know very few women who like the after effects of the tape ripping off a layer of delicate skin or their potential allergic reaction to the industrial strength adhesive.

Since a gag limits a person's ability to speak, make sure that you have a safe signal as well as a safe word for your scene. A specified number of grunts can work in some situations. Another idea is to have the bottom hold something that they can drop or wave to signal for emergency attention.

Stuffing fabric into the mouth is a hot idea. I personally think stuffing a pair of soaked panties into a helpless mouth is just juicy! Be careful with cloth with loose threads that might come loose and get inhaled. That's pretty awful. The same goes for any material that could be bitten off during teeth clenching passion and swallowed or inhaled. I'd hate to have to explain to the EMT why the girlfriend is choking on a plastic cock head.

Speaking of plastic cock heads, dildo gags are great! The dicks can be on the inside, outside or both. These are great for mouth stuffing sensation, erotic humiliation and the psychological charge of being turned into a human sex toy!

Hoods

Dear Midori,

I love hoods! Dominant women in bizarre hoods make my knees weak. Slave girls in tight hoods make me ragingly hard! Tell us more about hoods!

Bizarre Lover, Boston

Dear Bizarre,

I'll confess that the sight of a slave helpless and faceless in a tight and bizarre hood makes me really hot. The scene from the movie, Pulp Fiction, where the Gimp came out, exquisitely attired in a full leather bondage suit and a weird hood was a total turn-on for me. (Somehow, I don't think that's the reaction that the director had in mind, though.) This is why I have invested a small fortune in exotic head coverings, each one of them with their unique features.

Many kinksters like hoods for sensory depravation. Sensory depravation heightens the reactions to the remaining senses by removing others. Hoods can cut off sight, dull or block sounds, gag the mouth and restrict the movement of the face. Many hoods come with combined features such as removable gags, blindfolds, inflatable inner linings for a tighter feel and more. These features help increase the sense of being held captive, create helplessness and vulnerability and enhance the experience of deep submission. Many like the feel of mild disorientation caused by hoods as well.

Hoods work fantastically as bondage tools. I have several hoods with D-rings to immobilize willing victims. I even layer multiple hoods for better bondage and restriction. Once the slave's head is controlled, they're mine! Keep in mind, though, that you should never suspend people or support their body weight by the hood. This could lead to a fast trip to the emergency room or the morgue. Yuck.

Other hazards to keep in mind.... Unless it's an open face design, hoods can limit breathing. This gets worse as the person gets more and more excited with labored or faster breathing. The constriction of the hood and excitement can cause the face to swell a bit, or move inside the hood, sometimes blocking off those tiny air holes. Keep an eye on this. If the hood has an integral gag, use all the precautions I talked about in the gags section.

Some folks are claustrophobic to various degrees and find hoods anxiety provoking. Some like to have their fear pushed and anxiety brought up to feed the horniness while for others it's too scary or makes them freak out too much to have any fun. A hood can be a literal head-trip, so you really need to check with the person who's going to wear it. There are several hood designs out there that are easier for the apprehensive wearer. Hoods made entirely of mesh give the appearance and sensation of being hooded, yet the increased ventilation and visibility from the inside make them feel safer. The same goes for the strappy face cage styles, "Silence of the Lambs" style muzzles and half hoods like executioner's hoods.

Since the facial expression is hidden behind a hood, it's critical that the top be able to correctly interpret the hood wearing bottom's mental and physical state. Make sure that you know the bottom's body language and vocal cues in order to decide to press further in intensity, ease off or even stop the scene.

For many dominants and submissives, the hood is first and foremost an implement of psychological control. For both tops and bottoms, the dehumanizing effect of having your facial expression obliterated can amp up the fantasy of cruelty and the intensity of the scene. Imagine your sweet loving partner by day, now a dominant wielding a whip over you, but her face is hidden behind an ominous mask! This can make the role-playing hotter for the bottom too!

Hoods come in many materials - leather, latex, spandex, metal, mesh, neoprene, plastic, cotton, hemp and even converted gas masks. If you're dealing with a fetishist, naturally match the hood with the fetish. If you're into latex, a latex bondage hood for the bottom and a bizarre and scary looking latex hood for the top might be in order. Mr. S. Leather, Polymorphe and Demask make some of the finest hoods around.

Now, strap it on and go for it!

Japanese Bondage

Dear Midori,

I saw your book Seductive Art of Japanese Bondage *in the bookstore. What, if any difference is there between Japanese rope bondage and other rope bondage? .*

Rope Guy

Dear Rope Guy,

Don't you just love those beautiful Japanese lasses tied up with one leg is jacked up all akimbo? The look of lust and vulnerability just sends me! With the influence of the Web, Here's the mini version of explanation. Japanese rope bondage is the latest hot commodity in the dungeons across the country. Erotic Japanese rope bondage has its roots in Sixteenth century medieval Japan, where soldiers, warriors and law enforcement needed to know how to restrain prisoners. In the time of peace that followed, the Kabuki theater and Japanese erotic painters incorporated the images of bound heroes and captured princesses in to their repertoire of smut. Sex sells. What? Did you think Japan was just about cherry blossoms and good manners? My people are seriously sexually twisted under all that good decorum, thank you, very much.

Western erotic rope bondage styles that we're familiar with today sprouted within the last 100 years or so. The illustrators John Willie and Bob Bishop, photographer Irving Klaw and the ubiquitous model Bettie Page contributed to the style of rope bondage that we are familiar in the West.

Japanese rope bondage, or 'Shibari' is often extremely demanding on the body and mind. It's designed to reduce a person's mobility, although not always for complete immobility. It's also used to increase the sense of sexual vulnerability. After all, a bit of mobility only serves to deepen the sense of helplessness. Since its traditional military-based form may be quite harmful on most bodies, except the most fit and flexible, it's common to make adjustments to allow for the modern body and the principles of consensual SM. Western bondage with it's origins firmly planted deep in the wet cunt of sexual fantasies, can to be somewhat less harmful on the body.

The Japanese style often uses hemp rope, often rough on the skin. This is homage to the medieval images as well as for erotic sadism. Today most people used pre-treated hemp rope to reduce irritations. Often you'll see asymmetrical positions over a symmetrical body harness. You'll also see the rope seemingly messy. These visual and physical effects give the impression to the pervert voyeur as well as in the mind of the hot sub of being 'ridden hard and put away wet.' It just makes me horny just thinking about a hot girl in my rope bondage struggling with her cunt helplessly available! (But I digress...)

Fore more information on Japanese rope bondage, history and step-by-step how-to check out *Seductive Art of Japanese Bondage* from Greenery Press. You may also find useful any books containing images by John Willie, the movie *Wife to be Sacrificed*, *Klutz Book of Knots*, as well as a hard to find Japanese photo book called *Pleasure in the Fall.*

Stocks

Dear Midori,

I like the looks of those medieval wooden things to stick arms and head into. What are they called and how do I get them and use them?

Bondage Mike, Texas

Dear Bondage Mike,

They're called Stocks and they come from medieval Europe. Putting someone in stocks was a way to punish people with public humiliation or secure them for corporal punishment. I've been to many commercial and private dungeons that have varieties of them. I've had a couple in my own play space. They can be made of many materials like wood and metal. They have holes to fit the head, arms and legs of the person intended. You can make your own really simply with wood, a metal hinge, gate latch hardware and padding for the areas that touch skin. I've even seen folks incorporate stocks into the headboard or footboard of a customized bed frame.

If they're really heavy, having stocks on alone and nothing else will limit your bottom's movement. You can also attach the stock to other furniture. My stocks had eyebolts in it so I could hang them low from the ceiling, forcing my submissive to bend over and show me her goods. You can find stocks with combination arm and leg holes to force her down and spread her legs open for loads of fun.

If medieval implements of torment perk your fancy then you might find many of the illustrations from the book *The Instruments of Torture* by Michael Kerrigan, to be highly inspirational. Put your high school shop class skills to work! But make sure to adapt the design to kinky sex. The original designs were not meant to be fun, consensual or safe.

Have a great kinky time!

Medical Scenes & Nurse Fantasies

Dear Midori,

> *There was a photo spread set in a medical clinic in a SM magazine I saw recently. It really turned me on. I like a woman in a nurse's uniform, but I really want more than just the dress up. I get off to the fantasy of being examined and probed by a female doctor or nurse. Is this normal?*

Model Patient, New Orleans

Dear Model Patient,

The sound of high heels clicking on the clean white tiles, the snapping sound of a latex glove pulling on, humane restraints holding you down on the examination table followed by a cold metal instrument sliding into you as the beautiful yet strict doctor leans into you, telling you that you're here for your own good...

Medical fantasies are not all that uncommon, ranging from the simple naughty nurse misbehavior to the fully decked out medical interrogation and examination, even to the wilder end of castration fantasies. There's even a word for people who get turned on by having to undress before a medical professional – Iatronudia. While it's not right or nice to subject your unsuspecting and unconsenting medical professional to your sexual fantasy, there's nothing wrong with "playing doctor" with a play partner in your bedroom.

So, yes, you're normal. Don't worry about it. And why not find ways to enjoy it with another fun perv?

Often, the doctor's visit is the first and earliest experience that a person has around body control and modesty issues with a non-family member who has socially sanctioned authority over them. If you know what's good for you, you're going to do what the doctor orders, right? The anxiety and nervous energy that accompanies a medical situation as well as the fear of possible treatments can easily enhance sexual arousal for many. Some may have a scary incident in the past that they need to reenact and reclaim or a particularly pleasant one to recapture through fantasy. I knew one guy who lost his virginity to a hot and forcible nurse when he was a teenager. You can bet that incident shaped his fantasy world.

On the other side of the relationship, the idea of being the doctor and stripping a person of their power, exploiting their vulnerability and taking control, all in the name of "what's good for the patient" is a huge and sexy power trip for some dominants. Others enjoy the nurturing role taken to an extreme. The power dynamics, combined with the helplessness of the patient offer ripe material for sexual fantasies.

Since medical fetish and fantasies vary wildly from person to person, it's really important to find out exactly what you're looking for and what the other person wants. If one person wants an enema and a forced sperm sample collection from a buxom, horny urologist and the other person wants to do an alien captive experimentation and autopsy, there might be a slight conflict in expectations…. To say the least…

Other than the nature of the fantasy, you need to find out the extent of ambiance and equipment that's necessary for a hot scene. While some people are fine with just a simple naughty nurse outfit to get wood, many bedroom doctors and patients need as much realism as possible. They get off on the antiseptic environment, the scary looking equipment, the impersonal ambiance and glaring lights. Since it's not always possible to convert your den into a cruel chamber of medical horrors, you might want to consider renting a professional dungeon's clinic room…. Or convert the garage or back shed with some plastic sheeting as a drape, some linoleum flooring and a cot and you've got a battlefield medical tent.

Medical scenes enhance the erotic loss of body control and psychological loss of freedom through bondage and therapeutic procedures. There are companies that make legit hospital restraints that work exceptionally well for sex and medical role-play! After all, splints, casts and bandages are meant to limit a person's mobility.

Treatment devices such as enemas, catheters, sounds, urethral dilators, speculums and even tongue depressants serve as invasive control and a sort of bondage-from-within. After all, if you're filled up with a gallon of warm water, trying desperately to hold it in, you're under total control of the doctor. Many of these procedures are embarrassing and humiliating, making it hotter as the bottom's mind struggles between surrendering to the humiliation and maintaining their dignity.

If sensation and pain play is your thing, it can be a natural part of your medical scene. Electrical equipment for SM is often the same as physical therapy equipment, or related to it. Piercings make their appearance in the form of make-believe shots, and hemostats make great clamps. Sheep castration rings make for wonderful nipple clamps while the Wortenberg Wheel, no longer prevalent in the neurologists' office, is still pricking away in the fantasy clinic. Although some people get into activities that border on medical practice, such as saline scrotal inflation, most people are just happy as a clam with the make-believe.

Today there are many SM equipment vendors that sell medical or medical looking equipment. I'm sure you won't have any problems putting together the essential doctor's bag for your kinky examinations!

Pass the KY!

Good Resources for On-line shopping:
- www.kinkymedical.net
- www.sufferware.com
- http://rainbowrope.com
- www.stockroom.com

Electrical Play

Dear Midori,

In your recent column you had a great photo of a medical scene. You seemed to have electrodes coming out of various parts of that sexy girl's anatomy. Were they simply for visual effect or do you play with electricity? What's a good way to get into electrical play?

Charged & Ready, Detroit

Dear Charged,

Yes, those were electrodes. Some of them, like the ones on her breast were not hooked up to any devices but were there to enhance our fantasy that she was a helpless patient in the hands of me, the sex crazed mad doctor. The other electrodes, the pad on her labia, and the alligator clips on the metal speculum, they were real. I connected them to the TENS unit (Transcutaneous Electro Nerve Stimulation) and the ErosTek box. These are two different types of electrical stimulation equipment. These units caused a series of well-timed jolts, zap and throbs to run through her cunt... soon her juices flowed out onto the speculum that forcing her gaping lusty hole to open. The she started to quiver and shake... Good thing that I had her bound down with tight leather bandages and splints to the medical table, because in no time she was writhing and pushing against the bonds in waves of gushing multiple orgasms. Making her come without touching her, just with the subtle control of the dial is a huge turn-on for me. Like I said, I like to play the mad scientist.

There are lots of ways to play with electricity in kinky sex. The most basic electrical toys are vibrators. Electrical toys beyond the level of a vibrator need to be approached with caution and responsibility. The heart, ears, eyes and brain don't do so well with exposure to electricity. The potential for temporary or permanent injury and cardiac arrest, epileptic seizure, and more is a serious and very real concern. For this reason, many people prefer to keep electrical play "below the waist" as a general precaution. If you're new to this sort of play, it's a good idea to follow this guideline. Other concerns include skin burns and the deadening of tissue and nerves. Even with a milder toy such as the Violet Wand, overexposure to one spot can cause damage similar to that of a severe sunburn. It can also mess with the electrical field of watches and other electrical units like pace makers.

The Violet Wand, is a fun entry-level toy for many kink folks. It was introduced 80 years ago or so to cure all sorts of ailments from baldness to bad aura. It's a high frequency, low amperage generator, which creates a static-zap like sensation with beautiful arching electrical sparks that make the skin tingle. While you can get these from on-line auction and many other dubious sources, I advise you to buy yours from a reputable kink equipment dealer. The older ones have been known to short out or zap the top and the glass tubing may be quite brittle, leading to shattered glass during your scene.

Other toys like the TENS units are designed for pain management and muscle relaxation. TENS units are also available through www. stockroom.com. The Folsom Electric, ErosTek and Paradise Electro Stimulations are electrical units made for kinky sex play. They come with lots of cool tingling and throbbing attachments including pads, dildos, catheters, butt plugs and clamps and more. Most of the toys seem to be for boys but some are for girls and many can be modified to fit each person with varying degrees of success. They can also be a bit pricey. For cheaper toys, I like to use electrified fly swatters and remote control dog training collars as well. Again, keep it below the waist!

With a beautiful girl at my side, dressed sexy and wired for submission, I like to go out about town. Whenever I want to, I can press the secret button on my small remote control switch box and it'll send a jolt through her cunt. I can watch her squirm, wince and even come, wherever I want to! The most effective remote control unit I've found is from ErosTek. They are sold only through a few reputable venders. Mr. S in San Francisco and LA and the Stockroom have them as well

214

as large selection of various surface attaching and insertable toys for all genders. If you visit the Mr. S store you can even try them out(http://www.mr-s-leather.com). If you use attachments from other sources you may need to use some simple plug converters, which are easily available from electronic and stereo stores.

For an outing, I'd attach or insert toys of my choosing to my submissive. If you use insertable toys, it's a good idea to have your bottom wear something that keeps the toy in, such as pants, panties or a harness. Have the receiver unit worn in a pocket that's accessible for you, should you need to make any adjustments.

Have fun!

How to Be a Dominatrix

Dear Midori,

> *I want to be a dominatrix and get paid to beat men. I'm tall and strong and have been told I'd be good at this. How do I start?*

Bitchgirl

Dear Bitchgirl,

You go girl, with your badass self. Ok, let's see if you have what it takes to be a Professional Dominant. The better term to use is Professional Dominant. Dominatrix is really a dated term and it's so, well, tawdry and seedy. Also, professional dominants come in all genders, so it's better to use a gender-neutral term. The feminine form of this word would be 'pro domme.' (The last e is silent!) Here are the basics on getting started as pro domme. First you've got to know your kink stuff. Do you play with SM and D/s in your private life a whole lot with a bunch of different people? You can't just pick up a hot little outfit and a whip, put an ad out and call yourself a professional. If you don't have experience with SM in your private life, you are not qualified to take money from people. You'd be cheating them, in a sense. Would you want to eat at a restaurant with a chef who's never cooked?

The Pro Domme provides a great service, and SM can bring a person great joy and happiness. But if you do it without skill or psychological insight you may leave a person damaged emotionally, psychologically or physically. It's easy to hurt a person really badly with poorly practiced SM skills... and you can certainly kill a person with incorrectly done SM. Also, I have seen many women enter the profession without direct personal experience and passion for kink and come out of the biz very embittered about SM and men in general. You don't need that kind of pain down the road.

Remember that all or part of what Pro Dommes do may be illegal in your area. Think hard if you want an arrest record under many categories from prostitution, pimping and pandering, battery, practicing medicine without a license, running a bawdy house, sex crimes, and so on. Call some local Pros to find out. They can't give you legal advice, but they can let you know what the local mood is. You'll see them listed on the web and in local alternative papers. Once you've called them, you might want to get some legal advice through sex-work and SM positive legal professionals. Perhaps contact National Coalition for Sexual Freedom for some leads on a good attorney. Don't just go by rumors.

Next, you'll need space, equipment, wardrobe, a phone line, and some good ads. For wardrobe you'll want a selection of leather, latex, PVC, stockings, boots, high heels, corsets and other fetish wear. For equipment you'll need some good bondage gear, whips and other sensation toys. As you build up your clientele you'll find out what they like and what you'll want to invest in. Get a separate phone line and number. Space will be an issue for many. Some Pros like to see clients at home, while others want a separate space for privacy and safety. Many professionals share a space together. Find out where other Pros put out ads and place yours there. Good wording and a hot photo of you make all the difference.

Yes, there's a huge amount of money to be invested in this if you want to do this right. If you don't want to deal with all that capital investment up front, you might consider working or apprenticing for a 'house of domination' in or near your area. This won't protect you legally, but you get to find out what it's like with less of a time and money commitment.

Remember, though, that this is a business and a professional dominant is a professional entertainer. Basic work ethics apply. Show up to work on time. Answer phones when and how you promise to. Keep your client confidentiality. Do not be under the influence of substances or alcohol. File taxes. Keep your equipment clean. Keep your clients and yourself safe. Take care of your customers and keep to your boundaries.

Return customers and a happy healthy professional attitude is key to profitability as well.

If you don't have experience with SM in your personal life, don't even bother going pro. Get lots of experience first.

I get a lot of letters seeking advice for those wanting to be pro. The following is the form letter I send to them.

Before you consider becoming a professional dominant, here are questions to ask yourself.

- Do you play with SM extensively in your private life? (Most important)
- Do you have considerable experience in SM play with many different people?
- Have you bottomed a great deal in your private play?
- Are you CPR / first aid qualified and is your certification up to date?
- Do you consider yourself emotionally mature enough to handle psychological land mines that come up in SM play?
- Can you run your own business?
- Are you willing to open a business checking account?
- Are you willing to publish your name / address in a paper when you file your DBA?
- Are you vaccinated for hepatitis?
- Are you relatively well acquainted with basic human physiology?
- Can you retain a lawyer and a bail bondsman?
- Are you aware of the high overhead cost and capital investment of the business?
- Do you consider yourself to have strong boundaries, sexual and otherwise?
- Are you free of any issues with drugs or alcohol?
- Have you done any sex work before?
- Do you empathize with men?
- Are you willing to have a record of arrest in the worst-case scenario?
- Do you know what to do if a client stalks you?

- Do you know what to do if a client dies while in session with you?
- Do you know what to do if a client has a communicable disease?
- Do you know how to properly clean every piece of equipment you'll use for viral, bacterial and other sorts of exposure?
- Do you know what to do if a client tries to push sexual issues with you and tries to get you to engage in activities beyond your personal or legal limits?
- Are you able to separate your private life, your private play life and your vanilla life from your work?
- Do you have a healthy emotional support network of people who will know what you do?

I strongly suggest that you be able to answer yes to all or most of these questions before you consider going Pro.

Good Luck

Sex Slave

Dear Fetish Diva Midori,

I want to be my boyfriend's sex slave. Please tell me about what makes for a great sex slave?

Willing to serve in Minnesota

Dear Willing,

I can just see you naked,. greeting him at the door, presenting your dripping wet cunt as you kneel open legged... You're boyfriend is indeed a lucky man!

The first thing you'll need to do is to figure out what each of you want out of your sexual slavery to him. How long will it be? A night, a weekend, a week, a month or longer? Ask him what he wants out of his dream sex slave. Do his ideas match your ideas and what you want? Make sure to set your own limits ahead of time too... such as: the sex slave's duties will not interfere with work or work relationships. The sex slave will not be shared sexually with his friends, or only with certain friends, etc. The sex slave will not do dishes or any domestic chores, especially cleaning out the cat litter. . I don't know, what yours are, so I thought I'd bring up some that I've heard before from others.

Try to get as clear of information you can about what he fantasizes about. If he hasn't had clear fantasies about this or hasn't had a trained a sex slave before, then it might be hard for him to tell you the rules he'd like, so then it's your job to help him explore available options. Will you have a special sex slave name? "Slave girl" is ok, but how about something juicy like "open hole" "slut slave" or just simply a number like "9"?

How about special sex slave fantasy outfits that offer full access, like an open tit, open cunt and assless cat suit or teddy? How about a hot little maid's outfit with extreme heels? Maybe he'd prefer to have you shackled and captive, but just loosely enough so you can move to suck cock and get fucked. While you are his sex slave, will you wear a collar showing that he owns you for that time? The two of you will want to make sure to come up with a collaring ritual to indicate clearly when your slavery begins and ends.

Learn what signals he'll give you for executing sexual acts and what position he'd want you in for these. You may find things that he wants from you as a good sex slave to be embarrassing or erotically humiliating. You'll have to ask yourself, is what he's asking of you violates any of the limits you set, if you actually enjoy this and find the embarrassment makes you wet or if it kills the mood for you.

When it comes to specific techniques, whether for sucking cock or getting ass fucked over the dining table, continue to improve your skills and ask him for directions on how to do it better for him.

A great place to get dick hardening inspiration on sex slave games are smut stories and novels like the *Sleeping Beauty* series by Ann Rice and the *Marketplace* series by Laura Antoniou.

And in the end, this is a fun fantasy. So remember that you and your boyfriend are two equal, adult human beings engaging in a sexual adventure!

Dear Midori,

I've had fantasies of being the sex slave that you described in a recent issue. How do I go about finding the right guy that's serious about it, who knows what he's doing and with whom I'll be safe?

Hopeful slave girl

Dear Hopeful one,

You sound yummy! Hey maybe I ought to give you a 'spin' in my dungeon!

First, follow your instinct. If you like the guy that's great! But if you meet someone who seems to have all the cool toys and all the hot clothes and all the sizzling dominant lingo but your gut feeling says 'no' then back off and check him out for a while. One of the places that you might find a hot top for you to serve as a sex slave might be the local SM club. Go to http://www.darkheart.com/sceneusa.html for a list of clubs near you. It's a really good resource list. I also recommend asking the guy you're dating if the fantasy of having a sex slave might appeal to him. He just might like it! Why not make your own dominant from a guy that you're already hot for? Apart from that, I know many people seek their doms on-line. Flirting with people on-line is certainly fine, but it never replaces meeting them in person before playing. Be careful that many claim to be experienced dominants on-line but may have never held a whip in his non-virtual hands.

Once you join a local SM club, make lots of friends. These will be your helpers in finding a hot Dom for you. If your newfound kinky friends know your taste, then they can introduce you to prospective masters or warn you away from Master Bozo and Master Clueless. If you see a guy you're hot for at a SM party, watch him play and see if you like his style. If you want to know if he's serious, ask him about why he likes SM. Answers like "Because it's cool" "Because I'm a natural born master and you need to suck my dick" bode poorly. Run from Master Bozo as fast as you can. If he claims to be perfect, he's a turkey. Ask him about how he learned his skills and what technique he's particularly proud of. The good ones will go happily into details about their passion.

Then next big test is to mention your limits. You want a master who is understanding of your freshness to the experience and who will respect all your limits. He knows that he doesn't have to force your limits because you may be flexible with them as you gain experience and trust for him.

Letters to Slave Hopefuls

Open Letter #1 A simple letter to those who wish to serve a dominant.

Dear slave hopeful,

You are reading this letter because you have some notion that you want to serve someone, or you may even be considering serving me personally. Some of you have been in service and submission for several years. You may have had the honor of serving many glorious men and women. Some of you are just now considering entering the path of submission. You are all welcome to read this letter. Many of us dominants enjoy the well-trained servant, but also a nervous novice with genuine potential.

This wonderful world is filled with stellar dominant women and men. Like the stars in heaven, we each occupy a different part of the sky and shine in our own unique way. Each dominant is different and it is this difference that you should be celebrating. To serve a dominant well, you must understand her uniqueness. You must know what makes her tick, what pleases her and what displeases her.

Since you are reading this letter, I will stand in as the dominant in question. (If you are a dominant, please feel free to customize this letter as it suits your use.) I will share with you some of my basic requirements and expectations for slave hopefuls. Pay close attention, as you will be tested and judged. You will be tested by your actions, not your words, and I will be the sole judge. Remember, my world is not a democracy but rather a benevolent dictatorship.

Let's begin your education, shall we?

I expect a true desire to serve. There are people out there who claim to desire slavery, but they are simply wallowing in selfish fantasies. Many faux slaves come to a woman with a fixed idea of what slavery is... in other words, a list of exact expectations which they wish the woman to meet. Is this slavery? No, this is just fantasy role-playing between two people. But it's not even good fantasy role-playing because it's founded on a false representation. If role-play is what you want, then just say so. I love an honest role-play. I have a very different set of expectations for that. Above all I want the honestly of disclosure of intent. Role-playing is very lovely for a boyfriend / girlfriend, wife / husband pair. That, however, is not what I am looking for in a slave. If I wanted that, this letter would be titled "Dear Sweetie, Lets play some games this weekend. " But no, it's addressed to "slave hopefuls." My leather SM lifestyle is a very important part of my life. I do not have time in my life to waste on pretend slaves. I think that when a boy/boi/girl/grrrl is so demanding about exactly what they should get in a relationship with a dominant they are covertly trying to dominate in that relationship. This is a very distasteful situation and I cannot accept it.

Do understand, however, that I respect the limits of a slave. Also, I will listen to desires and curiosities as long as he understands that these are simply requests that I will listen to and may or may not act upon.

A sincere slave is willing to serve his dominant even if the task does not please him. In turn a sincere dominant will care for the slave's well being and contribute to his betterment as a person and as a productive slave.

Are you a sincere slave?
Or are you just a pretender?

I do not like manipulative game playing from slaves. I'm not talking about specific role playing games here. If we're playing 'naughty student' part of the rules of engagement is that the student acts up and the teacher gives a pretend punishment, all in the name of fun. I'm talking about poorly motivated boys and girls who deliberately do things to displease me, thinking that will earn my attention in form of discipline.

I do not operate that way. As I am a sadist, I consider the infliction of intense sensations as pleasurable and positive attention given to the slave. Why should I pay such pleasurable attention as punishment to misbehaving and manipulative brats? When I am displeased by a slave I take various privileges away from them or tighten protocols and rules of conduct. This may come in many forms depending on the offense or wrong doing. The punishment will always fit the offense in act and duration. For example, a slave may be told to spend time in the corner alone, he may be told to read a relevant book or write an essay with in a certain time frame, he may be made to redo many times over whatever task that he failed in until I am satisfied with the out come. The worst-case scenario is a permanent end to the relationship.

As mentioned earlier, slavery does not include specific role-playing games. If the boy or girl and I negotiate in *advance* about a particular role that includes misbehavior and resultant corporal punishment, that is fine... in fact, I really enjoy such scenes. For example, such a scene may be about a young maid that spills a glass of water or mouths off and is severely beaten with a hairbrush for the offense. As a fantasy scene, this is great, and a maid may ask me for such a scene. But the same maid, in service to me in real life, must expect that such an offense would be greeted with cold admonition. I hope you understand the difference that I'm talking about here.

I also expect a slave to be able to communicate clearly to me about all things. If a slave fails to communicate to me about a limit or a fear and I make him experience this, is it my fault that he feels awful? I think not. If a slave does not let me know that a task assigned is beyond his capacity and he feels punished unfairly, is it my fault? No. If he is having a difficult emotional day due to illness and I am pushing him physically, is it my fault that he felt worse? Of course not. In all these situations, had he communicated to me about the situation, I would have taken the proper considerations. Even the best dominants cannot train a slave properly if he does not communicate.... we are not mind readers. So it is a slave's responsibility to report everything to their dominants. Emotional transparency on the part of a slave is essential.

I expect grace, elegance and good manners from slaves. It is not only because I am a dominant, but also because of my upbringing that I expect basic good manners from those who are in service. A slave with poor manners reflects poorly on his owner. This must not be tolerated. If he is uneducated in manners, and is aware of that and if he is willing to ask and learn, I will teach him. But insolence, rudeness and foul language have no place in my world. If one is to be a gentleman or a lady servant, than I expect graceful and handsome manners. If someone is to be a feminine servant, such as a maid, I expect feminine grace and charm. They may be cute, sultry, shy, sweet, exhibitionistic, slutty, girly, quiet or chatty, or take another form of feminine expression, but never, ever will they be rude.

I expect a slave to be willing to expand his or her horizons of experience. A slave who never tries new things for me will bore me very quickly. This may require them to overcome some fears and anxieties. This, I fully believe, to be good for a slave's betterment. And I want that which belongs to me to become better in all manners. That only benefits all of us.

I expect the slave to take care of his health and well-being. If he is not well, how is he to serve me? I don't like a slave who is out of shape and is not making any efforts to change himself. I do not like slaves who drink excessively or use drugs. I despise unclean slaves. I cannot stand heavy colognes on slaves.

I expect a slave to be honest with me at all times.

Beyond basic demands and expectations, there are also several things that please me very much.

It pleases me when you pay close attention to my needs, desires and preferences. You should pay attention to what I like to eat, drink, do, and wear. You should know the colors I like, the movies I watch, the music I prefer. You should ask about how I like my tea for drinking or how I like my feet massaged. You should ask me how I want you to dress to please me. Eventually I will not have to ask, and tea will appear before me or my shoes will be polished and ready. You should pay attention to my cultural, sporting and non-kink interests. You should take the time to learn to pronounce my name correctly in Japanese. You should learn how I like to be treated when I'm ill, cranky, tired or stressed. These will be your most challenging moments of service.

You should learn how to care for leather, latex and footwear. A good servant is happy to care for my property and living quarters.

You may already know what gifts delight me, but more importantly learn what gifts I give other people, such as my friends, business associates and visiting guests. If you are able to select these well on your own you'll impress me far more then just presenting me with objects. Learn my standards of hospitality to others and practice it as you will be considered a representative of me.

Have enough sense to send me cards on my birthday, holidays and Valentines Day. My birthday is May 4th. Don't ever send me mediocre chocolates.

In general learn things that please me. You should learn to be a good conversationalist. Learn reflexology and other forms of massage to pleasure my feet. Think about what else you can learn and improve upon to better be in service to me.

If you have a particular fetish or like to see me in specific attire, save that for play time conversation. I am not going to prance around every day dressed for your fantasy. Don't act as if you deserve it and expect it. I have collected my extensive and expensive wardrobe over the last ten years for my own fetishistic pleasure, not yours.

Take the time to assess what talents you have that will be truly useful and pleasing to me.

Reflect upon the spiritual path of slavery.

Make your body appealing to me. Make yourself strong and flexible by stretching or taking yoga such that you'll be lots of fun for me to tie up in fun and exciting ways, should I choose to.

You don't have to be a masochist to serve me, but it helps. You must do your best to give your self wholly to me. Can you do it? How do you think you can best serve me and be trained? These are all things you must think about.

A relationship founded on SM and Dominance/submission is a complex thing that requires diligence from you. It's not a one-way street where you get treated and treasured in your shiny passivity. You're not some static toy I'm going to take down from the shelf. This is not easy and it is not simple. You must think deeply, feel honestly, and do the best you can despite fears and anxieties. Only then can you find peace in service and freedom in slavery.

You are given permission to ask me questions. You will, of course ask them politely, as I expect nothing less from you. By asking good questions and learning from the answers, you will be a better slave to me. Some time in the future, your questions will become minimal as you learn about me and what I demand of my servants.

I hope that all this was clear to you. You have much to think about now.

You are aware, I presume, that I travel a great deal. Can you still serve when the object of your focus is not within sight?

I look forward to hearing from you.

Here's to the beginning of service and learning....

To my future slaves....

Best wishes,
Midori

Open Letter #2. Further thoughts to those who wish to serve a dominant.

Dear slave hopeful,

Today let's discuss the concept of Transparency and Humility. Both are central to how I conduct my D/s relationships and Owner/slave dynamics, thus it's vital that you understand this. If you find that you do not agree with this, you should seek elsewhere to serve.

Transparency:

This means open and clear communication. This is important for all relationships but I believe it's carried out differently in different forms of relationships.

Let's break this down a bit....

First of all, clear communication requires self knowledge, maturity, the ability to assess one's emotions and then to put that into words. To state "we need to communicate" is easy but to actually do it can be very difficult depending on the match or mismatch of communication skills and development. Communication requires a lot of self-inventory, strong verbal skills and the ability to listen and really hear what the other is saying.

Some other factors that enter into communication compatibility (and down the road towards transparency) may be:

- Level of emotion based communication encouraged in one's childhood
- Levels of emotion based communication encouraged in one's adulthood environment
- Ability to empathize
- Sense of reciprocal empathy
- Gender bias (Not merely male and female but also masculine and feminine. Internalized gender biased behavior can even exist in same-sex butch-femme identified relationships.)
- Education (formal and informal) as this does influence the arsenal of nuanced language available to you
- Social position, community or what may be called 'caste placement'. I know this can be a touchy subject but different sectors of society do have different standards of acceptable emotional communication. Refer back to level of emotion-based communication encouraged in one's childhood and adulthood.) For example, during my time in the US Army, (I guess that's Camo-collared and military-industrial community), emotionally based communication was highly discouraged even in our friendships, whereas in among the academically inclined circle of my family of origin as well as certain people in my

229

current life, concise and articulate emotional communication is expected and treasured.
- Feeling safe in the behavior consistency of others around one.
- Perceived risk as result of communicating emotions.
- Level of investment into the relationship. (i.e. if it really matters to work hard on the relationship or not.)
- Agreement about terms and language. When I say "to serve," does that mean the same thing to you as "to serve"? Even in our leather community, with its highly codified language and terms it's hard to agree on just what simple things mean.

What other factors can you think of?

Now as to why I believe different relationships, including Owner/slave, have differently executed communication and therefore different transparency expectations...

- Equal life partnerships may have expectations of mutual and equal transparency and communication about just about everything...
- People only hooking-up for sex / play have expectations of communication only pertaining to that play. (Do you really want to know about all of someone's neurosis for a casual hook-up?)
- Parent to child: We expect (or desperately hope) that our little kids tell us everything. But most parents wouldn't dream of telling their kids EVERYTHING about their life and feelings. (i.e. Feelings about fight with your spouse are generally not shared with the child.) There is an appropriate disclosure level here.

So understanding the power dynamics and authority distribution in the relationship is key to understanding the flow of communication and transparency expectations you have in this possible relationship.

In my style of master-slave relationships, I do not believe that there should be an expectation of equal communication or mutual transparency. In fact, I believe that expectation of total equality in communication and emotional transparency in M/s relationship can be detrimental or damaging to the mutually agreed upon power discrepancy, discipline and training. The intent of the master is not always the concern of the slave. My intent is not always for you to know. Having said that, however, I believe in a master-slave relationship where the keen slave observes and understands the general goals and intents of the master through experience and executes obedience around that understanding. For a slave to ask 'why' is different then asking 'how.'

This perspective for me is specific to a Master/slave, service relationship and training relationships. It doesn't apply to fantasy role-playing scenes.

Another thought.... Transparency does not equal processing. For a slave to report his emotional state and life's activities does not mean a license to use the dominant, namely me, as a substitution for an emotional workout tool. As a friend of mine from the MasT (Masters and slaves Together) circle put it, "a good M/s relationship is impossible if the slave has not done appropriate processing before bringing the issue to the dominant. I don't think it's appropriate in any relationship to expect your partner to go through all of your processing with you ... You have to do your own inner work, talk it over with your support group, therapist, sponsor, whomever, maybe do some journaling.... and then, when you're clear on the issues & capable of communicating, you bring the issue for discussion. Complete transparency to me doesn't mean I get all of my slave's emotions spewed in my face each time they're having feelings."

I know this isn't a popular view with many... You might find that you don't like this either. Then we're not a good match and you should seek elsewhere. I'm not right for a whole lot of folks. I suppose that's why it's been so hard for me to find the right person to be in service to me. It's been a continual search. And as I search I continue to clarify and focus my philosophy, ideals, terms and conditions. (Unfortunately this focusing and narrowing down is making my search even harder! But I know it's worth it.) My Devoted One serves me in grace as I continue to look for that boy/boi/girl....

Speaking of my Devoted One, if you have any ideas at all that you want to be my one and only and everything, you're definitely not right for me. You have to understand your place in the household without the agenda of becoming a primary partner or something other then a slave. Harboring such an agenda would definitely go against the tenant of Transparency.

As with most people, I've had my share of difficulties and challenges in this arena. Often times it stems from a difference in expectations and a difference in what we think D/s words and terms really mean. I've made the error of assuming that because people are in the same community we mean the same thing when we express ourselves. It's my failure for going on this assumption. This hurts everyone involved and is frustrating. I've also experienced both sides of what it feels like when emotions are withdrawn because a relationship no longer feels safe. I've had a situation where I was in an emotionally traumatized state and discovered that the 'trusted servant' I counted on to be there for me wasn't capable of giving me the support I needed nor could she comprehend the pain I was going through. The servant's frustration in seeing and not being able to deal with my transparent emotional vulnerability turned into aimless anger and confused silence. I, as a dominant, then felt abandoned and lost my sense of trust in the servant. This can happen in D/s and M/s. How do you tell another person in a constructive manner that you don't feel cared for emotionally or feel that the other person doesn't have the coping tools you need? How does someone best hear such a message and then move forward to change the situation? You as a slave must be able to communicate your own feelings as well as understand that your dominant may have feelings that are difficult for you. If you cannot do these things, no amount of willingness or obedience will make the situation right.

Maybe it's not the transparency that's hard, maybe it's coping with the results that's the hardest part...

Humility:

Humility is the ability to objectively assess one's vulnerability and strengths. We tend sometimes to think of humility as putting oneself down. But to make a realistic inventory of ones flaws and talents and to grasp that in the scope of the larger population is to be humble. So, to put yourself down as 'worthless' is just as counter to the principle of humility as it is to be boastful and strut that you're 'hot shit.' Why would I, a woman of quality, want a property that's 'worthless'?

232

Humility is the ability to ask for help appropriately. To feel helpless and dependent on other's assistance is not humbly going about your way. To fail to ask for help because of ego or pride certainly does not come from a place of humility. A slave who doesn't know when to ask for help won't be able to get their duties done to acceptable standards. And what use to anyone, including to the slave themselves, is a slave who can't get reasonable tasks and obediences accomplished?

Where do you stand on these issues? Consider this carefully before you act upon a petition to serve me.

Midori

WRAPPING IT ALL UP...

So we've come to the end. We covered a lot of ground on SM, D/s, fetish, adventurous sex and passions that keep us alive and vibrant. As I write this, the very last bit of the book, I wonder if you enjoyed a peek into my mind and hope that you found something useful here. Writing, in its solitary act, often leaves us authors wondering alone about the effect our creations have on others. If you are moved to get in touch, I would love to hear from you about this book.

The essays selected for this book are just a small sampling of my writing. There's much more in waiting, should you like to read it. If so, please let Daedalus Publishing and me know that you'd like more. Maybe you have a topic you'd like me to write about? I'm open to suggestions so I hope you'll drop me a line.

Midori
Fire Horse Productions, Inc.
584 Castro St. #843
San Francisco Ca 94114
USA
Midori@FHP-Inc.com

The publisher can be reached at:

Daedalus Publishing
2807 W. Sunset Blvd.
Los Angeles CA, 90026
USA
info@daedaluspublishing.com

What am I up to next? Well, there are other books to finish, but most of all I have more adventuring to do! There are wonderful, exotic and surprising places - both on the map and in my heart - that I must travel to. I am continuing to travel all over North America, Europe and beyond, teaching classes, and in between I make sure to have time for my friends and lovers, for sports and other fun, and for my own soul.

I wish you and yours a joy filled journey of great sex, personal discovery, love and passion!

Midori

Photo by Steve Diet Goedde

About Midori

How can one capture the charisma and vitality that is Midori on paper? Midori is a champion of sex positive action, education, and adventure. Joyously, she practices what she preaches! Her unique blend of intelligence, style, experience, and hyper-sensuality is an inspiration to all who encounter her.

Wild Side Sex is the latest of the handful of books Midori has written. When Midori is not busy writing, she travels the world presenting to universities, undergraduate clubs, and the general public. Classes such as Aural Sex: Seduction by Voice, have sold out all over North America.

Raised in a feminist intellectual Tokyo household, she holds a degree in psychology from the U.C. Berkeley. She has written for many publications and books including, *Beauty of Fetish* and *Readings in Contemporary Sexuality*. Her work has appeared on HBO, BBC, *Mademoiselle, Penthouse, Playboy, Der Spiegel, Wired, British Esquire, Vogue, Surface* and many more.

Learn more about her education work: www.FHP-inc.com

-Linda Santiman, Editrix and fan

About Steve Diet Goedde

Steve Diet Goedde is a leading force in erotic/fetish fine art photography and has been a long-time collaborator with Midori. His work is lovingly collected in two hardcover books, *The Beauty of Fetish - Volumes I & II* (Edition Stemmle) in 1998 and 2001 respectively and the 2005 DVD anthology "Living Through Steve Diet Goedde". His work has appeared in countless galleries, museums and magazines worldwide.

Learn more about his work: www.stevedietgoedde.com

Carried Away
An s/M Romance
In david stein's first novel, steamy Leathersex is only the beginning when a cocky, jaded bottom and a once-burned Master come together for some no-strings bondage and S/M. Once the scene is over, a deeper hunger unexpectedly awakens, and they begin playing for much higher stakes. **$19.95**

Ties That Bind
The SM/Leather/Fetish Erotic Style
Issues, Commentaries and Advice
The writings of well-known psychotherapist and respected member of the leather community Guy Baldwin have been compiled to create this SM classic. Issues regarding relationships, the community, the SM experieince, and personal transformation, as they relate to this form of play, are addressed. Second edition. **$16.95**

SlaveCraft
Roadmaps for Erotic Servitude Principles, Skills and Tools
Guy Baldwin, author of *Ties That Bind*, joins forces with a grateful slave to produce this gripping and personal account on the subject of consensual slavery. **$15.95**

The Master's Manual
A Handbook of Erotic Dominance
In this book, author Jack Rinella examines various aspects of erotic dominance, including S/M, safety, sex, erotic power, techniques and more. The author speaks in a clear, frank, and nonjudgmental way to anyone with an interest in the erotic Dominant/submissive dynamic. **$15.95**

The Compleat Slave
Creating and Living and Erotic Dominant/submissive Lifestyle
In this highly anticipated follow up to The Master's Manual, author Jack Rinella continues his in-depth exploration of Dominant/submissive relationships. **$15.95**

Learning the Ropes
A Basic Guide to Fun S/M Lovemaking
This book, by S/M expert Race Bannon, guides the reader through the basics of safe and fun S/M. Negative myths are dispelled and replaced with the truth about the kind of S/M erotic play that so many adults enjoy. **$12.95**

My Private Life
Real Experiences of a Dominant Woman
Within these pages, the author, Mistress Nan, allows the reader a brief glimpse into the true private life of an erotically dominant woman. Each scene is vividly detailed and reads like the finest erotica, but knowing that these scenes really occurred as written adds to the sexual excitement they elicit. Second Edition. **$16.95**

Consensual Sadomasochism
How to Talk About It and How to Do It Safely
Authors William A. Henkin, Ph. D. and Sybil Holiday, CCHT combine their extensive professional credentials with deep personal experience in this unique examination of safety and erotic consensual sadomasochism. Second edition. **$17.95**

Chainmale: 3SM
A Unique View of Leather Culture
Author Don Bastian brings his experiences to print with this fast paced account of one man's experience with his own sexuality and eventual involvement in a loving and successful three-way kink relationship. **$13.95**

Leathersex
A Guide for the Curious Outsider and the Serious Player
Written by renowned S/M author Joseph Bean, this book gives guidance to one popular style of erotic play which the author calls 'leathersex'- sexuality that may include S/M, bondage, role playing, sensual physical stimulation and fetish, to name just a few. Second edition. **$16.95**

Leathersex Q&A
Questions About Leathersex and the Leather Lifestyle Answered
In this interesting and informative book, author Joseph Bean answers a wide variety of questions about leathersex sexuality. Each response is written with the sensitivity and insight only someone with a vast amount of experience in this style of sexuality could provide. **$16.95**

Beneath The Skins
The New Spirit and Politics of the Kink Community
This book by Ivo Dominguez, Jr. examines the many issues facing the modern leather/SM/fetish community. This special community is coming of age, and this book helps to pave the way for all who are a part of it. **$14.00**

Leather and Latex Care
How to Keep Your Leather and Latex Looking Great
This concise book by Kelly J. Thibault gives the reader all they need to know to keep their leather and latex items in top shape. While clothing is the focus of this book, tips are also given to those using leather and latex items in their erotic play. This book is a must for anyone investing in leather or latex. **$11.00**

Between The Cracks
The Daedalus Anthology of Kinky Verse
Editor Gavin Dillard has collected the most exotic of the erotic of the poetic pantheon, from the fetishes of Edna St. Vincent Millay to the howling of Ginsberg, lest any further clues be lost *between the cracks.* **$18.95**

The Leather Contest Guide
A Handbook for Promoters, Contestants, Judges and Titleholders
International Mr. Leather and Mr. National Leather Association contest winner Guy Baldwin is the author of this truly complete guide to the leather contest. Second Edition. **$14.95**

Ordering Information

Phone 213-484-3882
Email info@daedaluspublishing.com
Mail Daedalus Publishing Company, 2807 W. Sunset Blvd. Los Angeles, CA 90026

Payment All major credit cards are accepted. Via *email or regular mail*, indicate type of card, card number, expiration date, name of cardholder as shown on card, and billing address of the cardholder. Also include the mailing address where you wish your order to be sent. Orders via regular mail may include payment by money order or check, but may be held until the check clears. Make checks or money orders payable to "Daedalus Publishing Company." *Do not send cash.*

Tax and shipping California residents, add 8.25% sales tax to the total price of the books you are ordering. *All* orders should include a $4.25 shipping charge for the first book, plus $1.00 for each additional book added to the total of the order.

Over 21 Statement Since many of our publications deal with sexuality issues, please include a signed statement that you are at least 21 years of age with any order. Also include such a statement with any email order.